Good Writing

ALSO BY NEAL ALLEN

Better Days: Tame Your Inner Critic

Shapes of Truth: Discover God Inside You

ALSO BY ANNE LAMOTT

NONFICTION

Somehow: Thoughts on Love

Dusk, Night, Dawn: On Revival and Courage

Almost Everything: Notes on Hope

Hallelujah Anyway: Rediscovering Mercy

Small Victories: Spotting Improbable Moments of Grace

Stitches: A Handbook on Meaning, Hope, and Repair

Help, Thanks, Wow: The Three Essential Prayers

Some Assembly Required: A Journal of My Son's First Son *(with Sam Lamott)*

Grace (Eventually): Thoughts on Faith

Plan B: Further Thoughts on Faith

Traveling Mercies: Some Thoughts on Faith

Bird by Bird: Some Instructions on Writing and Life

Operating Instructions: A Journal of My Son's First Year

FICTION

Imperfect Birds

Blue Shoe

Crooked Little Heart

All New People

Joe Jones

Rosie

Hard Laughter

Good Writing

36 Ways to Improve Your Sentences

Neal Allen and Anne Lamott

Avery
an imprint of Penguin Random House
New York

AVERY
an imprint of Penguin Random House LLC
1745 Broadway, New York, NY 10019
penguinrandomhouse.com

Book design by Ashley Tucker

Library of Congress Cataloging-in-Publication Data is available upon request.
Hardcover ISBN: 9798217046959
Ebook ISBN: 9798217046973

Printed in the United States of America
4th Printing

The authorized representative in the EU for product safety and compliance is Penguin Random House Ireland, Morrison Chambers, 32 Nassau Street, Dublin D02 YH68, Ireland, https://eu-contact.penguin.ie.

NEAL:

For Eddie and Kent

ANNE:

For Sam, Claire, and Jax Lamott,

my pride and joy

Easy reading is damn hard writing.

—Thomas Hood

Contents

Read This First

I FIRST WROTE PROFESSIONALLY FOR A NEWSPAPER IN New York's Hudson Valley. As a cub reporter at the *Kingston Daily Freeman* in the late seventies, I cut my teeth on town meetings, county court, the police blotter, and obituaries. I learned to obey the front page's tight style restraints: omniscient third person, complete sentences, no exclamations or questions, sixth-grade vocabulary, scarce adjectives or adverbs, pretense of objectivity, inverted pyramid, few parentheticals, no slang, no alliteration or rhyming, no long quotes, stricture after stricture straitjacketing my weirder impulses. The result? Efficient, economical, and colorless language. I had a lot to learn about writing, and in retrospect the overly mannered style of hard news was a godsend to a mind that had spent its youth immersed in literary and experimental fiction, where rules are to be broken and anarchy is always knocking.

One morning, my editor Sam Daleo looked me in the eye: "Neal, the trick is to write with your verbs." He explained the difference between a vivid verb and a weak one. Thumb forward in this book of rules, and you'll see that as Rule 1, with an explanation for how and why it works. In my mind, it's the Daleo Rule. And for a long time, it protected and encouraged me.

I was happy with my one rule of rhetoric and persuasion, and my career progressed at a steady pace. I became a better and better newsman in terms of fact-gathering and reporting. My writing didn't look so different from what I scanned on the front pages of *The New York Times* or *The Washington Post*, at least to me. And then one day I woke up to the *Times*'s front-page story on the marriage of Prince Charles and Lady Di.

Here is how *New York Times* political writer R. W. Apple Jr. revealed the spectacle in his second paragraph: "The 2,500 guests inside Christopher Wren's Baroque masterpiece, St. Paul's Cathedral, the hundreds of thousands who watched the wedding party ride in magnificent horse-drawn carriages from Buckingham Palace to the cathedral and back, and the 700 million television viewers around the world witnessed a fairy tale come to life: the handsome Prince Charles in naval uniform marrying the lovely 20-year-old Diana Spencer, daughter of an earl, amid the sort of splendor the modern world has all but forgotten."

This syntax didn't emulate Tom Wolfe or Hunter Thompson in a magazine displaying the New Journalism that was all the rage. It wasn't a feature story masquerading as an eventful occurrence. Here stood a hard news reporter packing information into one elegant phrase after another, and I trembled in shame. Where did the legendary Johnny Apple learn to do that? He was thinking differently from me about newspaper writing. For both of us it might be a craft, not an art, but he showed without telling that daily journalism could be graceful and as beckoning as literary fiction.

By a couple of years later I had accumulated three or four rules of rhetoric, enough to survive in the medium-sized newspaper where I now worked. The *Bergen Record* in Hackensack, New Jersey, had a circulation of 150,000, but because it catered to some of the richest people in the state, it landed on the doorstep with a thud, fat and thick with advertising and a wide-open news hole overflowing with local and wire reporting. The newsroom employed 260 editors, reporters, feature writers, illustrators, opinion writers, cartoonists, photographers, clerks, and librarians, a number more typical of papers three times its size. Among the sixty or so writers a few stood out as stylists. I dissected their stories and occasionally asked for advice. By the time I left five years later, I had corralled another five or six rules.

Think about that. A meager six or eight rules of rhetoric could maintain a career, and ten were enough to be admired by peers.

That's the germination of this book. From my time at the *Record* through a corporate career in publicity and marketing, and into a third life as a spiritual coach and author, writing has stood fast as my default expertise. I've made a living from magazine writing, business writing and editing, speechwriting, copywriting, short story writing, ghostwriting, memoir editing, scriptwriting, presentation writing, and book writing . . . and all along my hack writing career, I have quietly expanded my kit bag of rules for good writing. The bag contains thirty-six now, which doesn't mean I'm three times the writer I was in the eighties. I still can't conceive of arriving at Johnny Apple's second paragraph all by myself. But thirty-six rules are more than enough for me to amuse myself with complex sentence puzzles every time I sit at my keyboard. These rules don't restrict me so much as they encourage me to stretch into more and more possibilities, leaps of imagination, and lovely explorations.

Thomas Mann defined a writer as someone for whom writing is more difficult than it is for other people. Most books are not composed by people whose primary concern, expertise, and profession is words and rhetoric. Most books are written by academics, other experts, or pundits. Many fiction writers, some of them quite successful, are less concerned with their sentences than with moving the plot along. For many authors, the main interest is the overall theme they are elaborating or the argument they are proving. But for some professional writers, the central interest always remains the sentence. Next comes the consistency or flow of the material. The topic or plot of the book, the content of the speech or lyrics, takes third place—just the material with which to exercise persuasive prowess. Throughout my careers my default comfort with writing, and especially the improvement of sentences, has consistently shown up. Writing remains my professional practice. And it is exactly the same to me whether I'm writing a news article, a business letter, a novel, or a self-help book. My job is the sentence, and secondarily the paragraph or flow, and only thirdly the content of what I have learned or am learning. Writing is a vehicle for my life to play out. We all have our masteries, a job or avocation that fulfills our social destiny as a groove—often for income and pleasure, but even more so as our field for personal exploration, for finding out about life. A garbage collector on a sanitation truck explores freedom and routine and how people live, and with luck has afternoons free. Writing is like that for me; it mirrors what I've explored up to today, and reflects where I'm now standing. Oddly, I'm not often conscious of that interplay; when I sit at my desk, shaky or confident, it's for a job. All I anticipate is the difficulty and reward of composing good sentences.

And yet.

As any decent writer knows, we don't write what we *want* to write. In my case, that would be a novel with the erudition and voice of William Faulkner. No, we grudgingly write what we think we *need* to write, which means that most of us, including Barbara Kingsolver and Ian McEwan possibly, are stuck with writing about something we haven't completely gotten over.

In that sense, all books are, to their authors, memoirs—

reorganized diaries of what has been guiding them, or calling them to explore, or keeping them up at night. After my private clients and I had been examining the mechanics of the inner critic for a few years, I decided to make a book about it, titled *Better Days*. I'm a writer; it's my default job.

My writing rolls along as a vehicle to explore my world. My study happens to include as one of its subjects the very possibility of elegance in articulation, using the tropes and rules of my upbringing. In one sense, writing well is the same as articulating well is the same as exploring carefully. But an academic who writes badly is also exploring and articulating well enough. The academic is following her own fascinations in worlds of tiny discriminations and hair-splitting analysis, her own playground far afield from mine. In my world of writing, I hair-split infinitives, not outside discoveries. As long as I'm aware that my being a writer is an arbitrary default, no better or worse than being a garbage collector or academic, I'm capable in my job: to produce good sentences.

So this isn't a book about becoming a writer, or how to write, or syntax, or rhetoric in the philosophical sense. Annie and I aren't grammarians or the usage police. You won't meet epistrophes or ablative absolutes or master plots. This book is curious about what happens *after* you've got a sentence in mind, maybe even after you've put the thought to paper, maybe after you've finished your entire first draft. This book is concerned with improving sentences. The book embraces *persuasion* in its biggest sense—not to win an argument, but to be elegant, to convince a reader to continue on to the next sentence, and maybe to persuade them that a song fills the air even if the subject is poisonous frogs of Costa Rica.

And while we call them rules, these suggestions engage at first as tips. After trying them out, you might adopt some as useful for your prose. Only then do they become rules, and only temporarily in your mind. We humans have enough rules already; new ones should be added cautiously and lightly. Some of the rules in this book won't work for you or your way of writing; then ignore them. Troll us if you must, but believe it when we say we don't mean to be scolds.

Anne's take:

ALMOST SINCE MEETING MY HUSBAND, NEAL, IN 2016, I was aware that he had compiled a list of thirty-six rules of writing, based on his years as a journalist. They were at once simple and obvious but also profound. They were pretty much all you needed to know when you set out to make sentences, and seemed especially useful if you had gotten something written and were trying to make it better.

I started handing them out to random writing students, and then eventually had my pupils go to his website, where they are still displayed. And I internalized them, so that in the nine years we've been together, I've called them up like a checklist when I edit my work before handing it over to

Neal for his input and response. Stronger verbs, layered sentences, twist those clichés if you are going to insist on the right to use them—I'd run Neal's list and make sure I had not committed any of his sins.

My teaching has mostly been about the attitude of writing: gaining the confidence to get your stories told, to stop *not* writing, to tell the truthiest truth, make the plunge into empathy, and, mostly, to develop the habit of keeping your butt in the chair every day. Neal tends more toward encouraging people to write better sentences and paragraphs. Hence this book, and my own fixation with the best possible sentences I can write.

My beloved friend the great food writer M. F. K. Fisher said, "Write one good clean sentence and put a period at the end of it. Then write another one." That is great writing advice, but so much easier said than done. Let me give you an example:

> My mother walked quickly toward me, across the
> Irish-green lawn, looking at me in a very angry way.

Neal would have a field day with that one if I had included it in an essay (and he would also discourage me from using "having a field day" or any other cliché, like "easier said than done" two sentences above).

He would return this to me with my weak verbs questioned ("walked," "looking"), the "very" crossed out, and the

"Irish-green" challenged. Now the sentence would read "My mother stalked across the lawn toward me."

Or: "Sometimes you need to spread your wings and take off no matter how shakily from the hard ground on which you stand, and fly; but other times, when things are very weird and scary, you need to find some kind of weighted ballast, to secure you here." Now, I think that is a perfectly nice sentence, but when I showed it to Neal, it came back "Sometimes you need to lift off and fly, but in times like these you need ropes and ballast."

He took out the excess verbiage, the "very," the adjectives and adverbs, and voilà, the one clean sentence M. F. K. Fisher asked of us.

One day I got curious what he was up to over in his office, and he explained that he was turning these insights and tips into a book.

Well. Hmmmph. I had written a book on writing once, and thought maybe two writing books in one family might be a little unseemly. Then I started reading it. I loved what he was doing—not simply listing the rules but making sense of them in his often quirky way. Then in my own hemming and hawing, butting-in fashion, I offered my take on some of what he'd written, tiny little suggestions on points he might want to add or delete, and he shot me a look such as one might make upon seeing a ticket on one's windshield, flat and annoyed.

Frantic to save the marriage, I coughed up yet another

idea: What if I annotated what he had already written so brilliantly?

This suggestion drew a slightly different look on Neal's face. "That might work," he said.

So I have gone ahead and added my two cents. If you knew Neal, you would think me quite brave. But to be fair, he has done the heavy lifting; I am the water boy. Together we've described everything we know about writing better sentences that you might find useful in your work.

I'd like to add briefly that ever since we met, we have collaborated on each other's material. Collaboration, which we'll talk about throughout this book, is a pleasure and a great relief, working with a trusted fellow writer to raise your work to its highest potential. A colleague can save your bacon and reputation—you don't want to burn any bridges by sending off work to a boss or agent or editor that is not your best—and the give-and-take can make writing a little more relaxed and playful, like playing doubles instead of singles in tennis.

I might ask Neal to tell me everything he knows about spirit, say, or Buffalo Springfield, or Gatsby, or mulch, and I'll scribble down his answer word for word, and then steal it all, frequently without attribution. (He knows he is so doomed without me that he must let this pass.) Or I will hand him a solid second draft to read, and he will return some time later with a marked-up copy, with notes like "The lede is weak. Consider starting with the graf near the bottom of page two." Or, similarly, "The ending sucks," or at least that's what he's saying if you read between the lines. He'll cross out adverbs, make suggestions for stronger verbs, and shift things around. And I do exactly the same for him.

So far, the marriage has survived. Almost every writer needs a partner who can look at your work with fresh eyes—you are either going to be bored with your work by the second draft and need encouragement and/or advice, or, worse, think it's just fine and quite ready to send off to your editor that moment. But you'll regret not taking a second look. The words may be fine, but a first draft isn't enough. We're after *really* good, and the best each of us can do.

So herewith are Neal's best rules and advice on how to write better sentences, with my commentary, experience, and encouragement. I hope his tips help you as much as they've helped me, both to become a better writer and to keep getting a kick out of the process.

RULE 1:

Use Strong Verbs

Replace weak verbs, which are imprecise ("walked," "stood"), with vivid verbs, which are specific ("trudged," "malingered").

GOOD OLD SAM DALEO. SOMETIMES THIS RULE IS EXpressed as *Write with your verbs.* Weak verbs are limp fish, sapped of energy by overuse: "Walk," "feel," "think," "dine," "talk," "tell," "use," "get"—all colorless. "It felt bad to him" doesn't do much for the reader, nor does "He walked out of the house." Prosaic words, whether verbs or other parts of speech, leave readers unsteady about what is being conveyed. When I question my first bad attempt, more colorful actions—"His stomach churned" and "Rushing out of the house, he tripped on the last step"—magically appear.

Writing with strong, vivid verbs yields new sentence structures. It's not just bland to say, "He walked out of the house." It also doesn't lead anywhere much. But once I've got him "rushing," I imagine a consequence, the foot tripping on the last step, which gives me the puzzle of how to manage two verbs in one sentence. A more complicated but eminently readable sentence structure emerges. As I question my lackluster wordings and try new things out, my sentences mix up; some reel out longer while others sit boldly simple. The reader won't be lulled into a soporific monotony of one subject-verb-object sentence after another.

The more specific the verb, the less likely you'll need an adverb. "Raced" doesn't require "quickly." "Meandered" doesn't require "aimlessly."

By the way, don't confuse this rule with the unrelated grammatical distinction between "strong" (irregular) and "weak" (regular) verbs.

Like any rule, you can take *Use strong verbs* too far. By avoiding the obvious verb "won," sportswriters imbue the victorious high school team with the courage and skill of Roman gladiators: The opponents typically have been slaughtered, massacred, blasted, blitzed, blown away, clobbered, thrashed, blanked, thumped, walloped, whomped, whipped, flattened, shellacked, crushed, hammered, shafted, or vanquished. Poor kids. Poor parents.

Anne's take:

A STRONG VERB IN A SENTENCE INSTANTLY IMPROVES your writing. If no word springs to mind to vividly describe the action in your sentence, use your online thesaurus. Don't use "run" when you can use "sprint," "race," or "scurry." A verb describes what the subject of your sentence is doing: "The dog atc our Thanksgiving turkey." (This really happened ten years ago.) But Bodhi did not "eat" the turkey. He devoured, gobbled, wolfed down, and inhaled our Thanksgiving turkey. Bad dog.

"His grandfather sat on the porch, carving a figure out of a thick twig." OK, close your eyes and look at the screen on the backs of your eyelids. You see the old man—the noun—and what he is doing—the verb: carving something, holding it in one hand, slicing off thin layers of wood into a shape he has in his mind, to be revealed. But what if your sentence read "His grandfather slouched on the porch, whittling"?

Or "We tried to handle a week without Internet" could be "We hunkered down for a week without Internet." "Hunker" is a great verb. Try to use it more often. "The gorilla lowered her body to the ground" could also be "The gorilla hunkered down."

Here's another one: "She could not stop thinking about eating an entire chocolate cake." What about "She craved chocolate cake"? "Crave" is a great verb because it is so precise, so psycho-visual. You know that exact feeling when you've been in that state, longing for and obsessed with eating your body weight in cake, and then doing that—gobbling or devouring or wolfing it down. Cake is to me as turkey is to Bodhi.

Or "She went out to the garden and got a lot of vegetables for the meal she was cooking that night." Why not "She gathered vegetables for dinner"? "Gathered" rings with its suggestion of arms embracing lovely things—vegetables, flowers, little kids.

"Slouch," "whittle," "hunker," "crave," "gather"—these verbs are exact and rich. The reader immediately sees and understands the action you are describing—which could also be "The reader gets it."

RULE 2:

Question "Being" and "Having"

The verbs "to be" and "to have" are the weakest of all; by nature static, they slow a narrative.

"TO BE" AND "TO HAVE" AREN'T JUST OVERUSED; THEY'RE barely verbs. They suspend the sentence in an inert universe. Think of the sentence "I am _____." Whatever fills in the blank is fixed in place and time, frozen. "I am tired." "I am happy." "I am a teacher." "I am a jerk." The object of such a sentence characterizes you, or identifies you, or describes you. Most verbs move me along; "to be" keeps me in place. Any forward motion that the reader has been chasing slows to a full stop.

English reflects the odd behavior of "to be" by declaring that sometimes the nouns on either side of it can both be nominative, which means that they don't quite separate into subject and object. It's called the predicate nominative, which you don't need to remember. Lemon is a fruit. Shirley is a doctor. The sentence describes an equivalence rather than an action. Other languages reflect the outlying position of "to be" by ignoring it. In Sanskrit, if two nominative nouns appear without a verb, then "to be" is assumed. You don't have to bother to write it down to complete a Sanskrit sentence. This emphasizes how the idea of "being" lacks the typical propulsive energy of a verb.

Likewise "to have" does not describe an activity, but an acquisition that took place before the sentence began. "I have three dollars." "I have a sister." "I have a basket full of trouble." "I have" means that I already acquired the thing that I am naming. The thing is a possession, which is a little like an identity. If I think I own something, then I have stopped it in time as if it is neither in development nor in decay. Both of us—the reader and the object—are immobilized by the sentence.

Two exceptions to the questioning of "to be" and "to have" are common. One, they can be useful helper, or auxiliary, words, especially in constructing passive sentences. While "I was running to the store" might be replaced by "I ran to the store," you probably wouldn't want to turn "I am running for president" into "I run for president." Two, they can help me sound authoritative. In the next paragraph, I use a declarative sentence with the verb "to be"; "Becoming is an activity; being is static."

If you know a little about Hinduism, then it makes sense that Sanskrit has two verbs for "to be." One, *as*, is nearly as static as the English "to be." But the other, *bhu*, carries a liveliness that often doesn't make it into English translations. When a form of *bhu* is used in the Hindu holy work the *Bhagavad Gita*, for instance, it implies "becoming" as well as "being." Becoming is an activity; being is static. Using *bhu*, "I am a man" has hidden in it the notion that "I am becoming a man," and probably "A man is becoming me," as if identities aren't resting places but developmental transitions. The language itself unfolds a distinctively non-Western notion of things in constant flux. English is not so subtle in its hidden metaphysics. We Westerners are confirmed materialists. Things "are," and what you see is what you get.

You might ask, "What about Hamlet's soliloquy?"

"To be or not to be, that is the question. Whether 'tis nobler . . ." The entire speech runs thirty-three lines. The first fourteen lines include *nine* occasions of the verb "to be." Hamlet punches it out almost exclusively with one- and two-syllable words. Then he makes a course correction. The final nineteen lines include *one* occasion of the verb "to be," and that one an auxiliary verb ("Is sicklied o'er . . ."). More three-syllable words appear. Hamlet's language rings with more authority, or ego, in the opening section than in the longer analysis of the situation, and that might remind the reader that a person of Hamlet's age is caught between the chop of childhood impulse and the gather of reflective adulthood.

Anne's take:

YES, NEAL IS OVEREDUCATED AND A LITTLE WOO-WOO but he did *not* get the above distinction off a box of Celestial Seasonings tea: he got a master's in Eastern studies and had to learn Sanskrit during the first year of Covid. (He did not actually "learn" Sanskrit, per se, so much as study it online with twenty other masochists at his alma mater.)

What he is trying to say is that you can do better than "being" and "having." Question yourself each time you use either. See if you can find another verb that adds something to the sentence for us.

"I was tired" might become "I grew tired." Growing tired is active. "I was tired" is flat and, well, tired. That sentence needs a nap.

"I have some money" might become "I found some coins between the couch cushions," every child through history's main income stream. The new sentence blossoms specific and evocative. Or, in my case, "I took some cash from my husband's wallet." (We live in a community property state.)

Or "I pocketed some money by using coupons, while people in the express lane glared."

The great E. L. Doctorow wrote, "Good writing is supposed to evoke sensation in the reader—not the fact that it was raining, but the feeling of being rained upon." And as Neal said, "to be" and "to have" are static, which is OK when that is the condition of the subject. But part of good writing is teasing readers to want more, to keep turning the pages because the story and descriptions are alive, not passive or inert.

When you are finished with a section, take a break. Then go through your material again to see how often you've settled for what Neal calls "barely verbs." Pin each one to the corkboard of your mind and stare it down until an action word pops up that communicates something.

RULE 3:

Keep It Active

Pay attention to words that end in -ed or -en and are preceded by a form of "to be," and watch out for -ing endings; try flipping the sentence to get it more active.

THE RULE OF THUMB IS TO FAVOR AN ACTIVE VOICE OVER A passive voice. In practice, this is thornier than grammarians would tell you. They stick to a view that -ed and -en verbs (and some others) preceded by an auxiliary verb are the culprits. As far as they go, this is true and worth examining. Watch what happens when a passive sentence is transfigured:

> I was handcuffed by Jim.
> Jim handcuffed me.

> They were buried by the avalanche.
> The avalanche buried them.

We know by ear which sounds stronger, or more appropriate. Musicians are said to play by ear or by reading scores.

But they're always playing by ear. The discordant note, whether identified on a score or imagined as an interval in the mind, sounds the same. Symphony conductors don't instruct players on the score's notation; they conjure up scenes in the musicians' minds—a picnic on the rocks of a windswept beach, a falling-out with a close friend—and ask the players to translate scenic emotions into melodic, harmonic, and rhythmic sounds. By ear.

Trust your ear. But also use pointers—rules—to find fault and improve.

If the passive voice is inferior, why does it exist? Sometimes the passive voice is superior, and must be kept. Let's take our first example above. If the context is a detective untying Catherine, he might ask, "Who did this to you?" Catherine might answer, "I was brought here by Jules, but I was handcuffed by Jim." The correct usage of the passive voice is to put a special emphasis on the object of the sentence, usually the person or noun found at the end of the sentence. "Jules brought me here, but Jim handcuffed me" slightly deflates the word "handcuffed," and separates Jim as possibly the more culpable.

Generally, "My mother watched over me" is better than "I was watched over by my mother." But if I were distinguishing parents, and making the case that my father was neglectful, the second version might work.

> Passive: "I was silenced not by the librarian, but by the person I had a crush on."

Active: "The librarian didn't silence me, but the person I had a crush on did."

The second version is weird. It doesn't work.

Grammarians distinguish the passive voice from verb forms that use participles. That's a fancy way of saying that -ing verbs are not considered passive. But often they might as well be, sounding flabby or inert. The -ing ending blows up a verb, allowing it to become a noun (*swimming* is fun), or an adjective (I put on my *swimming* cap), or part of a direct action (I'm *swimming* in childhood photographs), or—what we're talking about here—adding distance to the narrative, often implying a prior action the same way that the passive -ed and -en forms do.

We previously showed how "He is running for president" can't necessarily be replaced by "He runs for president." But that's the exception. Try these:

"He was running by the bank when the robbers emerged." Hmm, wonder what those guys are doing there?

"He ran by the bank. Right then, the robbers emerged." Oops! Wrong place to be.

The first has a singsong tone. By questioning the -ing verb, which is in all other ways appropriate, I'm led into a more staccato, direct, active phrasing, which adds tension and danger.

Anne's take:

YOU WILL NOTE ABOVE THAT NEAL SAYS TO BE CAREFUL of verbs ending in -en, but then he forgot to mention any. When I thoughtfully pointed this out to him, he coughed up one: "The soufflé was eaten by the dog" versus "The dog ate the soufflé." I might add the backstory: "The eggs were beaten vigorously for the soufflé" versus "She beat the eggs vigorously for the soufflé."

These examples hardly matter—who even makes a soufflé anymore? But the point is that when the subject of the sentence receives the action instead of performing it, the sentence is weakened by your choice . . . Wait, wait. "The sentence is weakened" is in the passive voice. "You weaken the sentence" is better, although I do not want you to feel bad about this. Good writing is about taking each sentence and making it as strong and true as you can.

Of course, there are many circumstances in which the passive voice works. It is famously useful for those attempting to avoid responsibility for tragic decisions, as in "Mistakes were made."

You might legitimately backload a sentence to build up the drama, to pack a bigger punch. President Franklin Roosevelt used it at the start of his "Day of Infamy" speech: "Yesterday, December 7, 1941—a date which will live in infamy—the United States of America was suddenly and deliberately attacked by naval and air forces of the Empire of Japan."

I have always found this to be an interesting and touching decision, placing the emphasis on the 2,400 citizens and personnel who died that day, rather than on the evildoers. He stirs our hearts before moving on to anger and action.

The late, great Douglas Adams begins his sequel to *The Hitchhiker's Guide to the Galaxy* in a perfectly used passive voice:

> The story so far: In the beginning the Universe was created. This made a lot of people very angry and has been widely regarded as a bad move.

That he does not say *who* created the universe makes this so much more mysterious and quirky. This casual thing happened—the universe was created, like so it goes. *This* is what matters. Notice that "has been widely regarded" also is passive, which adds a distinctly wry tone.

As Neal says above, pay attention whenever you use the passive voice, and see if your sentence might be stronger if you switch to the active. "The sentence was changed to be more muscular" versus "She changed the sentence to be more muscular, and to win dour Neal's approval."

RULE 4:

Stick with "Said"

When attributing a quote, "said" is the default verb; the reader's attention is on who said it, not how it was said.

"SAID" IS ENOUGH. "CHUCKLED," "SMILED," "RANTED," "explained" . . . all of them are too much. Don't look for synonyms, and drop explanatory adverbs from attributions. This is one time to favor a weak verb.

"Said" is enough because the quote is what's important. The verb accompanying the attribution—"said" or "chuckled"—is expected but not registered, like prepositions and other word- and idea-connectors. "Said" has a mechanical, grammatical function and isn't intended to project a particular meaning. It's a weak verb that doesn't need to be replaced.

This rule was first taught to me by newspaper editors. If you can still find one, grab any newspaper's front page and skim through the quotes. You'll see "said" "said" "said" "said" ad nauseum, and nary an adverb accompanying it.

Newspaper style prefers an unopinionated, objective tone, devoid of interpretation. By reducing all attributions to "said," the rule removes subtle bias that invades synonyms such as "claimed" (which inserts the author's skepticism) or "argued" (which suggests a defensive stance). While other writing may allow interpretation and bias, the rule is still handy as a default. Notice that you're probably adding drama with your attribution; do you want to be so overt all the time? Why not let the reader interpret the character's statement all on their own? Maybe you can use "said" most of the time, reserving embellishments for special occasions.

Anne's take:

MANY VERBS TO REPLACE "SAID" SOUND LIKE THE EFforts of a person whose first language was not English. "Chuckled" is the worst of all. Never, ever use "chuckled" in place of "said." But I challenged Neal on this rule, as there are a number of synonyms I am fine with: "stated," "announced," "remarked," "observed."

He responded by calling me a Philistine.

We have not spoken since.

But isn't "responded" the appropriate verb here?

And "whispered" is a great verb, meaning the character is avoiding being overheard, and much better than "said quietly."

"Mumbled" contains both "said" and the adverb "indistinctly" in a nice package, but if you use the latter, you have to worry that Neal will go off on one of his tirades about the use of adverbs. I would risk it: "Mumbled" tells us in seven letters that the listener may not have caught what the speaker was saying.

The main thing about a long patch of dialogue, which I don't mind in the right hands, is that you cannot keep saying "he said," "she said," or "they said," because it begins to sound staccato, but by the same token, you can't substitute a desperate synonym, like "asserted," "avowed," or "contended."

At the reader's end, we need to know who is speaking at each point in the conversation. At your end, you need to present dialogue in such a way as to not annoy Neal.

RULE 5:

Don't Show Off

Let others be erudite; your job is to befriend your reader.

AS MUCKRAKER JESSICA MITFORD FAMOUSLY INSTRUCTED, murder your darlings. (The pedants will point out that she was quoting a now-obscure lecturer and writer from the early twentieth century named Arthur Quiller-Couch.)

Your darlings—your carefully crafted cleverness and erudition—run the danger of cracking your book's seamless world if it's fiction, and being relegated to the style-over-substance bin in nonfiction. Readers are suspicious. They've read too many books, seen too many TV shows, where someone did or said something clever but so out of character that it ruined the experience. Show-off authors are as repugnant as show-off classmates in grammar school. In a third-person novel or a nonfiction work, the hidden narrator/author has to retain a consistent voice and thought pattern. If your narrator has a propensity to riff philosophically, those meanderings deserve human believability. A roughneck narrator isn't likely to spout a perfectly formed description of a caterpillar becoming a butterfly. Save that lovely metaphor for your next book, and a dreamy, clichéd character who can use it.

The French essayist Blaise Pascal was brutal: "Everything that is written merely to please the author is worthless."

No gimmicks, said the great short story writer Raymond Carver. Don't shortcut your responsibility to describe a character's psyche by introducing a dream that coincidentally addresses his driving fear. Minor characters who are fortune tellers, shrinks, older brothers, or ex-girlfriends often serve the same contrived purpose. Don't have him live in the basement of the Empire State Building unless it's a novel about living in the basement of the Empire State Building. Don't have her swim in the ocean and suddenly hear a dolphin speaking cetacean to her unless you're writing about Atlantis. Assume seamlessness and then protect it. Get rid of anything that stands out or exists only because it shows everyone how good you are with words.

A very high percentage of people who read books seem to value being right about things. That creates a problem: Do I aim my nonfiction treatise at an erudite audience that is by default skeptical or at the common person who doesn't need proof? Or somewhere in between? Your subject matter will sometimes answer that. If it's a technical manual, then it's a narrow audience. If it's a textbook on an arcane subject, likewise. But even for those, it might be a good idea to try to satisfy the erudite using the logic and language of the great middle.

As a newspaper reporter in the mid-eighties, I developed an expertise in AIDS and women. After HIV first rampaged through the gay men's community, it found its way into female sex workers through bisexual men and addicts sharing needles. The women who were dying from AIDS lived on the margins of society, mostly out of sight, and so weren't heard from much. As I've mentioned, I wrote for a suburban paper in a well-heeled, highly educated suburb of New York. My readers were accepting of a sixth-grade vocabulary, mostly, but they also seemed to appreciate it when an article resorted to words like "epidemiology" or "vascular" or, by then, references to "Kaposi's sarcoma" or "longitudinal metrics."

The subject matter was still fresh when I left the newspaper and freelanced for a supermarket tabloid that catered to women's issues, and a less-educated audience. I reinterviewed my old AIDS sources and produced a longish piece on HIV's spread into vulnerable women, keeping it to a sixth-grade vocabulary and simpler sentence structures. You know what? I got everything across that I had before, without any big words or catering to the college-educated, and this time to an audience who first learned about AIDS and women from me.

Anne's take:

THE FIRST REVIEW OF MY CAREER WAS A HIT JOB BY *Publishers Weekly* that arrived in the mail from my agent. It was for my novel *Hard Laughter*, which followed my father's brain cancer and our family's response. Some of the book read deep and sad, while some of it was funny in a gallows-humor way. The review said that its meager charms were outweighed by my frequent "show-offy overkill."

Luckily, I was still drinking at the time.

Of course this was devastating to my self-esteem, but you know what? It guided me through the next nineteen books. That phrase, "show-offy overkill," has rung through the chambers of my mind ever since, and on the last draft of everything I write, I go through and cut any flagrant efforts on my part to sound more erudite and charming than I actually am, as well as my more forced efforts to use irony or witticisms to leaven tough emotional moments.

You have to push back your sleeves and get tough with yourself here. It may hurt you to cut any lines, especially the ones that thrill you, but it will hurt even more when a reviewer beats you up for being a show-off.

If I notice early on that you are a brain and are trying to prove this to the rest of us, I am probably not going to read much further. If your book gets published and all sorts of overeducated types are talking about it with excitement, and I end up with a copy, I will leave it around so that guests will think I am brainy. I will pick up enough from these conversations, plus a few major reviews, to pretend that I read and enjoyed it. Then I will insist that someone who is visiting take it with them, and they will, because they will want to seem smart, too, and they will leave it out so that their own visitors will comment on it. They will have gotten enough out of what I said about it to hold their own in conversation and will deposit it on one of their visitors, and then we will both be done with it and can get on with our lives, reading books that tell marvelous stories that we find entertaining and can follow.

RULE 6:

Prefer Anglo-Saxon Words

Favor shorter, punchier Anglo-Saxon words over fancy, abstract Latinate words.

PART OF NOT SHOWING OFF IS DEFAULTING TO COMMON language. Some words seem more physical and are usually preferable to their abstract synonyms. Pick the Anglo-Saxon word over a Latinate one, when you can: "crash" over "collision," "hurl" over "propel," "dockhand" over "stevedore," "smelly" or "rank" over "malodorous" or "pungent." As readers, we prefer to come across the immediate and concrete over the learned and remote. Anglo-Saxon language is conversational, while the Latinate lexicon tends to the academic. Which makes sense, since Latin itself derives much of its usefulness from being dead. Without the corrupting influence of Western cultural changes, Latin has long claimed the title of *lingua franca* (originally a pidgin French-Italian mishmash developed by the Crusaders). It is the precise, incorruptible language of medicine ("gluteus maximus"), botany ("binomial nomenclature"), zoology ("homo sapiens"), science in general ("condensation"), philosophy ("a priori"), writing ("capitalization") . . . you get the picture. It's helpful in academic research and professional training to have a single-minded, seldom-changing set of words that can cross linguistic boundaries. If literal meaning were enough and logic ruled over all forms of truth, then Latinate words would delight authors and readers alike.

But we are three-centered beings. We live not only inside our minds, but also within the sensations of our bodies and the emotions of our hearts, which define their own truths. As a long-specialized language, Latin tends to omit the body and heart. Of course Latin didn't when spoken by early Romans ("Stick it in your *glutei maximi*, centurion!"), but in the ensuing centuries the subtleties have been left behind as Latin accepted its role for sharing technical, practical knowledge.

What does it mean to read and write with the body and heart as well as the mind? Words evoke sensory feelings and emotional memories. If a car crash lived only in my intellect, I might get away with the sentence "Newtonian laws of motion proved true when John's automobile disassembled." Instead, I say, "John's car was totaled," and a picture of a heap emerges in the mind's eye, a sinking feeling in the belly, and a sympathetic gloom in the heart.

Political speeches often lapse into a kind of imperial jargon that long ago fell into the scrap heap of irony. "It behooves us?" No. It's our duty. "My distinguished colleague." No. My opponent. "Enhanced interrogation techniques." No. Torture.

The English language is full of brilliant Anglo-Saxon and Anglo-Saxon-ish short words that give sentences a staccato urgency and a personalness. They show up slangy and often slightly off-color, which excites the body and heart. "Sweaty" versus "perspiring." "Car" versus "automobile." "Boring" versus "tedious." Latin resonates in long drones and la-di-da singsongs, which eventually tire the reader. No matter how detailed the scenery, descriptions needn't devolve into a technical manual. Punch them up. Have a heart.

My favorite exception to this rule is the song written by Don George for Duke Ellington in 1948: "You're Just an Old Antidisestablishmentarianismist."

The Argentine short story writer Jorge Luis Borges pursued a different take on this rule, in part at least because his writing branches into the philosophical. He said that he preferred writing in English to his native Spanish. Why? Because unlike Spanish and other languages that are either Germanic or Romance, English retains both heritages, and often presents words that are more physical (Anglo-Saxon, Germanic) paired with near-synonyms that are more abstract (Latinate, Romance). One of the pair of words inevitably fits into a particular sentence more securely than the other. He offers several examples—think about a sentence in which one of the pair rings truer—"regal" versus "kingly," "fraternal" versus "brotherly," "obscure" versus "dark," and "spirit" versus "ghost." Borges liked the choices in part because he saddled up to abstractions even while the physical action galloped along.

Anne's take:

I DROPPED OUT OF COLLEGE AT NINETEEN TO BE A WRITER and since then I've gotten old and funny. As a result of those two developments, I had to look up the difference between Anglo-Saxon and Latinate words. Neal tried to explain above, but let me restate what he said: Anglo-Saxon words are typically short, simple, and specific, whereas Latinate words are longer and more formal. "Job" versus "profession," "end" versus "terminate," "light" versus "illumination."

I once came upon a useful quote from Ward Farnsworth's book on rhetoric, *Farnsworth's Classical English Style:* "For most people most of the time, attractive English isn't the art of choosing beautiful words. It is the art of arranging humble words beautifully."

The fanciest words I ever used were in my first novel, *Hard Laughter,* when I believed all good writers periodically used esoteric, formal words that they'd probably found in a thesaurus, with many syllables and a hint of the BBC. My dad, who was a writer, read the first draft and convinced me to use humble words instead, twenty-five-cent words instead of silver-dollar words. But I, like every writer I've ever known, am a mixed grill of ego and low self-esteem, and for a long time tried to get away with silver-dollar words so you would think I was more educated than I am. I'd use words like "hillock" that I'd found in the thesaurus, for small hill, or "presage." Do you even know what "presage" means? Well, a few of you and my husband do, but a lot of us only sort of know what it means and have to go look it up. OK, it means a sign or warning of something probably bad about to happen, but if you are choosing fancy words that I have to look up, the bad thing that is going to happen is that I'll stop reading your stuff.

Shirley Jackson said that a confused reader is an antagonistic reader. Neal is right—use our wonderfully juicy, earthy, familiar Anglo-Saxon words. And for the love of God, never, ever use "terminate" for "end," or "perspicacious" for "astute" or "shrewd."

This is a true story: I read the word "petrichor" on the first page of a book that I was auditioning at a bookstore. Raise your hand if you know what it means. (Not *you*, Neal.) It's a beautiful word for the distinctly earthy smell when it rains on dry soil, which I discovered after I looked it up on my smartphone. Now, while I love that smell, and loved being reminded of this scent and the first rains in the fall, having to look it up made me feel dumb, which does not make me want to continue reading (that is, buy) the book—possibly yours.

RULE 7:

Sound Natural

Unless you're writing a technical manual, keep your language conversational and use modern speech patterns.

IF IT SOUNDS LITERARY, IT ISN'T. OUR AGE IS CASUAL, and overly formal usages—the King's English and all that—disturb the reader the same way that stiff English translations of foreign works make some people uneasy. We like our idioms, our pop culture, and common words that share our everyday hopes and fears. Formal writing may objectify the focus, but it also adds distance between the writer and the event being described. I don't welcome an obvious narrator, omniscient or otherwise. I prefer absorption, as if I'm being guided through a jungle, not a zoo with glass cases and bars.

Most fiction writing nowadays has a character-decided point of view. Whoever's voice is front and center is the temporary narrator. That technique demands verisimilitude. The character talking or thinking or narrating has to be consistent with what you've learned about their physical description, background, and idiosyncrasies. All that individual color can be lost in the abstraction of an externalized narration. Formal writing is so universalized that character has a hard time emerging.

Elizabethan English belongs to Shakespeare, not you or me. I was twenty-four when Laurence Olivier appeared on my TV accepting his honorary Oscar. Listen to this jaw-dropping sentence: "In the great wealth, the great firmament of your nation's generosity, this particular choice may perhaps be found by future generations as a trifle eccentric, but the mere fact of it—the prodigal, pure, human kindness of it—must be seen as a beautiful star in that firmament which shines upon me at this moment, dazzling me a little, but filling me with warmth and the extraordinary elation, the euphoria that happens to so many of us at the first breath of the majestic glow of a new tomorrow." That one sentence took up more than half of his speech. Maybe you think highly of it, which is absolutely OK. To me, it was overblown, formal, and noncolloquial, and left me judging Olivier pompous in his self-deprecation. That's how literary-style writing can damage trust, at least for some of us.

Anyone can accidentally slip into formal, literary writing. It looks right, seems erudite, has a certain glow, but it's flat-out wrong. When Annie and I read each other's pages, the code for "You're losing me with this flamboyance" is "Maybe a bit much?"

Stiff, formal language has its rare, carefully adopted place in contemporary writing, particularly in light comedy and historical fiction. Herman Wouk's brilliant first novel, *Aurora Dawn*, set in the early days of Madison Avenue when soap operas were on radio, adopts the seventeenth-century novelist Henry Fielding's voice throughout, even beginning each chapter with a summary like this one from chapter 7:

> In which the reader has the privilege of meeting Talmadge Marquis, reigning satrap in the industrial realm of Soap, and learns more of the truly fascinating history of Aurora Dawn [a soap brand]; but which he may skip if he is only following the love story.

Political speeches can get away with a little formality, particularly at the top. "Friends, countrymen, we meet in this solemn moment," and so on. But the temptation to continue with lofty and florid patterns is usually worth resisting. Some wag in the audience is snickering, and others are questioning your sincerity, and maybe your bow tie.

Anne's take:

THE LAST THING I WANT FROM A NEW BOOK IN MY HAND is for it to feel intentionally literary. I want to step into a world that the author has carefully crafted, where I can get lost and, thus, found. If I feel the author is trying to impress me with their literariness, I'm going to put the book back on the shelf.

The horrible reality of being a writer is that you have to get the reader to keep turning the page. To use the more literary term, you need to suck them in. You do this by establishing a trustworthy voice that attracts attention. Whether you've composed a novel or a biography of Lawrence Welk, the reader has picked up your book planning to accompany you for a few hundred pages, and they may recoil if your voice sounds highfalutin or snobby.

When I was coming up, a number of writers engaged in literary pyrotechnics—John Updike comes to mind, but he was uniquely gifted and I won't hear a bad word against him (except that he had tiny, tiny problems envisioning fully realized women characters). Tom Robbins was flashy—not elegant like Updike, but so funny that I forgave him everything. Barbara Kingsolver does not sound literary, nor does Mark Twain, but both are entirely committed to the sentence, and such brilliant storytellers that they create an elevated sense of flow, without sounding lofty.

If I notice you trying to sound literary, I'm out of here. You can have a snobby, affected character who speaks in a formal or courtly way, who comes across as either touching or a fool (or both) and that is obviously OK. But using effete words and phrases so you will sound more exalted is a turn-off. Just tell me your damn story with the best, truest sentences you can muster.

RULE 8:

Trust Your Voice

Your natural voice has its own tempo, pitch, ease, and overall sound. Let it ring out.

MY FIRST LITERARY HEROES WERE PHILOSOPHICAL AND moody, full of self-examination and streams of consciousness. How disappointed I was when my own writing voice turned out to be nothing like that, emerging light and curious mostly, conversational and often good-humored. I was compensated, though. Soon after discovering my true voice, with its fatal lack of profundity, I realized that I never had to try so hard anymore. My true voice comes out on its own. The trick became finding all the ways to disguise it within other people's personalities. Fortunately, I'm a bit of a chameleon, which might be what gives me a light voice in the first place.

A writing voice is a little more complicated than a singing voice. It has its own sense of melody, harmony, and rhythm, but this voice also has coveted interests, a personality, and sentences it wants to get out. It emerges with practice. Your writing voice isn't created, but discovered.

When you're in your own voice, neither imitating nor preferring another, you're allowing yourself to riff, and edit later. You might wish that you had a different voice, but any other voice you adopt is immature and relatively ignorant of its place in the world, or even how to behave.

Trust your voice—the nexus of all the decisions you make as a writer: topic, point of view, diction, syntax, metaphor, imagery, even formatting—and go with it.

What we call a writer's voice projects from the writer's quirkiness. We love how each of our favorite authors thinks differently from others. Each writer draws on their idiosyncratic set of fears and wishes, and we follow along appreciative of the author's fresh set of eyes. In fiction, the writer's voice and quirks define the conflicts and revelations that show up in the pages. Most characters are a constellation of flaws, but only the flaws that a particular writer cares about. The characters we root for are who we want to become, but only by aligning with the writer's confidence that their own interests are universal.

In nonfiction, the writer's voice is likewise partly determined by their quirky interests and partly by their overall personality. Is the nonfiction writer sarcastic, breezy, grave, worried, light, heavy, curious, provocative, distant, expansive, and on and on?

Like music, writing relies on the integration of melody,

rhythm, and harmony. We're adept at all three, but usually one is prominent—your default talent. Can you find your hidden Beatle? Are you Paul, pure melodist? John, a rhythmic harmonist? George, a harmonist? Or Ringo, a rhythmic melodist?

Melody is the bright or dark stuff, the words that sharpen into wit or aphorisms or telling detail. Metaphor is melody: It provides instant recognition, meaning, and access to truth.

Rhythm is pulse or drive. It may have a beat, but the trick is to flow naturally without hitting the snare drum. This isn't the 4/4 or 6/8 rhythm of meter, of iambs or dactyls. It's the feel that provides lulls and punch lines and, when appropriate, staccato disruptions.

Harmony is the glue of tonality that is by nature relational and emotional: It might feel friendly in its casual, conversational way, or harsh in its threatening coldness. Harmony is recognized in the layers that amplify or correct each other, the complications of character or difficult logic that allow us to recognize that this story, this argument, is as garbled, clear, contradictory, and transparent as the jumble of our everyday lives.

As in all things, pay closest attention to your strengths. Wallow in them. Let them spin slightly out of control. And recognize that your so-called weaknesses aren't. If you're not a natural melodist and your metaphors won't sing out, don't break your spirit trying. An ordinary or imperfect metaphor is worse than no metaphor, always. No one will notice that metaphors are missing if your drive or your heart are quirky enough, and I promise they are. Amplify what you do naturally, and the reader will be pleased.

The trio of melody, rhythm, and harmony correspond to the three-centered human, a concept that shows up in spiritual works, especially after the Russian mystic G. I. Gurdjieff elaborated on it in the early twentieth century. Melody is the head center, playful and curious, illuminated and spacious. Rhythm is the body center, active and functional, dancing. Harmony is the welcoming heart, corralling two or more voices, relational and loving. If you think about it, even as lyricists Paul and John kept to their archetypes. Paul's lyrics tend to be open and playful ("Silly Love Songs"), and John's about the challenges of relating in the world ("Help! . . . I need somebody").

It often takes years of writing practice before your true voice comes to life. Malcolm Gladwell famously says that 10,000 hours of practice in any endeavor yields a sense of flow and mastery that has the feel of switching on cruise control. That was my experience. After years of dogged reporting and roughly 10,000 hours of writing and rewriting, one day I sat down to write a short story, and it wrote itself for me in forty-five minutes. The story was populated with light and feathery thoughts, a natural arc, and an innocence and sincerity that bubbled out. I take no credit. My first reaction was "Crap, this doesn't look like Faulkner at all." But from that day on, writing has been easier.

You can write just as *well* without having found flow and a sense of voice, but not as *easily*. Learning to write is like learning chess. Thinking mechanically, sorting out all the possibilities two or three moves ahead, is how chess goes for a long while. But if you play enough games, and maybe study openings in a book, you might suddenly find yourself thinking four moves ahead. It isn't that your brain has sped up and found a way to factor more computations in the same time. It's that you've switched from seeing individual moves to registering common patterns. The patterns let you skip over a lot of fruitless possibilities. In writing sentences, that means your brain is skipping over a lot of clichés, flabby choices, boring structures, and confusing words, and is happily searching for rare and new strategies down the line.

Anne's take:

NEAL SAYS I'M PAUL, A MELODIST WITH LOTS OF BRIGHTness and surprises, metaphor and humor. But Paul is my least favorite Beatle, plus Neal and I went to see him last year at the Oakland Coliseum, and we both got Covid. So I'd like to be John. By the same token, I'd like to write like Barbara Kingsolver or Virginia Woolf. Neal says Kingsolver is John, a rhythmic harmonist, with a dense, massive score peopled with lots of instruments, colors, and heart. Woolf is George, somewhat distant but yearning, disruptive because she is a truth seeker, appalled by what she sees, capable of shouting but not interested in it.

There is just one problem. If I try to write in Kingsolver's or Woolf's style and voice, I not only sound like a fraud, I've become a fraud. My work plummets. When I was thirty and had published three novels, Isabel Allende's international sensation *The House of the Spirits* was published in the U.S., and I started trying to emulate that rich, vivid magical realism. (Also, since my father had been dead for six or seven years, quite out of the public eye, I hoped to retool him as a Chilean freedom fighter.)

Magical realism in Petaluma, right? Crazy lights and ancient smells popping out of the toaster, along with the bagel?

At some point, I accepted that I could write pretty well in one certain way, and I think that Neal was right that I'm a Paul. The greater message is that we each need to find the literary abilities where we feel comfortable. That's our default place. Of course you can reach for the stars and try to soar as an experimentalist, but to be honest, I probably won't want to read your work.

So find your own truest voice and style and play it the best you can. You'll know if your rhythm works when you read it out loud, literally using your voice. Maybe sentences aren't landing, or seem to dangle, or come to an awkward end. Even worse, it sounds like you're just running a lot of words together and there's no real shape to the sentence. The paragraph is losing speed or energy. If needed, you can fool around with the rhythm by putting the stress on other syllables. Commas and pauses are rhythm.

Harmony is you filling out the picture if it is too thin. Do you need to mix in some local color? Can you add counterpoint? This might include minor plots or multiple storylines, where one is about psychology, one about plot and detection; the first might be darker, the second lighter. Create tension between multiple voices in dialogue. You are creating richness, sweetness, layers.

An editor will help you figure out which elements of song are missing when the time comes, and that will be easier if you have stayed true to your own sheet of music, to your story and characters and themes. In the meantime, never forget what my friend Randi Mayem Singer preaches: "Tell me a story, make me care." And never forget that steady Ringo is there in the background all along like a heartbeat, a pulse: boom-boom, rat-a-tat-tat, oomph, a crack from the snare drum, a sandy whisper of drum brush from the quiet side of things.

RULE 9:

Question Transitions

Transitional phrases ("then," "next," "when," "meanwhile," "however") are not needed unless a gap in time or logic has opened.

SEVERAL OF THESE KIT-BAG RULES REINFORCE THE PRINciple to say more with less. Word economy doesn't just ease the reader, it often forces out blunders. Noticing extra words can reveal weak verb constructions, provide a gimlet eye to adjectives that might be made redundant by a better noun, and clear a path to forward motion that has been interrupted or slowed by draggy clauses.

The most common transition, "then," as in "Victor then placed the knife on the table," seldom improves on its omission. A reader is aware of time passing and assumes that what follows in text also follows in time. If I don't need a word, I get rid of it.

This ability of the reader to trail along naturally without prompts doesn't just apply to time. In logic, too, the reader can be trusted.

> John raised his arm. When the teacher called on him,
> he hesitantly stammered out his usual wrong answer.
> On cue, his classmates broke out laughing.
> Fortunately for John, the teacher called them to order.

That might become:

> John raised his hand. He stammered out another wrong answer, igniting the class into an eruption of snickers and laughs. The teacher rapped her ruler for silence.

The reader knows that raising a hand results in being called on. "When the teacher called on him" is an unnecessary transition. "On cue" is another. And anyone with a heart recognizes that the teacher's intervention is "fortunate for John."

Watch for paragraphs that start with parenthetical clauses, such as "While Roger blabbed on, John stumbled in." They feel tentative to the reader, as if the author is backing into the picture. While it's true that too much *in media res*—starting in the middle—is dizzying, it's also worth noting that too little is insulting. Watch for any paragraph that starts with an adverb followed by a comma. A friend threatened to write what she called a psychedelic Western that would open with the sentence "Suddenly, bullets." A more typical example: "Unexpectedly, the washer overflowed." An overflowing washer is never expected. Test whether the logic of the story is enough to carry the reader on without the superfluous clause or word. When I was a newspaper reporter, Joe Gemignani, a memorable editor, scanning one of my rushed and skeletal reporting jobs, called out, "Ah yes, the all-powerful 'Meanwhile.'"

Also think about removing adverbs that act like transitional phrases but simply add an authorial interjection. Most uses of "actually" can be removed, as well as such phrases as "So far as she knew . . ." or "Showing good manners . . ."

Anne's take:

FOR ME, THE MOST IMPORTANT TRANSITIONS HAVE TO do with the passage of time. In old movies, we watched the hands of a clock spin around and around, or the pages of a daily calendar fly out the window, but you can't show this on the page. You can think of your own cool ways to make time pass. If it hasn't been long, you could say, "She had made a decision by the time the light turned green" or "the bread had fully risen," or "When he had finished the last of the haggis, he struggled to his feet." If real time has passed, the leaves outside the window have turned red, or fallen off, or just begun to bud. The dog's muzzle had gone gray, or the narrator's beard. The baby left for college, or she found herself midway through her master's program, or (in my case) "She married the love of her life three days after receiving her first Social Security check."

"Easter came early that year" lets the reader know that it

is now March. "Labor Day couldn't come soon enough for the harried mother, who frequently questioned whether she should have raised orchids, or teacup poodles, instead of children." And so on.

Neal says that most uses of "actually" can be removed, but I say *all* uses of "actually." Thirty years ago, a friend pointed out the extreme overuse of "actually" in both the spoken and written word and ever since, I hear and see it everywhere. It is a tic of the writer or speaker. Once you start listening for it, you will hear it everywhere.

> "How are you?"
> "Well, actually, I'm doing pretty well."
> "Have you ever been to Alaska?"
> "I actually haven't."

Use the "find" function on your word processor to root out "actually," but for what it's worth, I don't mind "meanwhile." It is most often used as an adverb, meaning at the same time or during the time in between this or that event—"I am going to Norway this fall. Meanwhile, I am bingeing on Scandinavian noir."

In its guise as "meantime," "meanwhile" can also be a noun—it's two, two, two mints in one: "In the meantime, elections have become billion-dollar processes." It has been used as both since the 1300s, and Neal comes along and announces that we shouldn't use it? You decide: Seven hundred years—plus of recorded use, or cranky, wiseacre Neal?

RULE 10:

Link Ideas with Semicolons

If two sentences are tightly linked and one progresses from the other, consider separating them with a semicolon.

A SEMICOLON LINKS TWO COMPLETE SENTENCES; IT reinforces and seems to prove their connection. This oft-neglected tool glides in effortlessly. It's a beautiful way to reflect without adding a transitional phrase. (The semicolon's other use as a super-comma is more on the grammatical side of things; we won't go into it here.) As a rhetorical device the semicolon is unlike any other: It creates a sliding pause, as if the sentences on either side would be less without their partner.

See what happens when I replace a period with a semicolon:

> My eyes are green, my hair red. For Halloween I usually dress as a six-foot-four leprechaun.

> My eyes are green, my hair red; for Halloween I usually dress as a six-foot-four leprechaun.

The semicolon acts as a knowing gesture, tucking the second thought into the first.

If you're anti-semicolon, that's all right, too. Many writers refuse to use it in either Rule 10's way or as a supercomma. A tweener of questionable birth, the semicolon makes them uncomfortable.

Anne's take:

I LOVE SEMICOLONS. THERE ARE SELF-RIGHTEOUS PEOPLE who secretly think that the semicolon is a hybrid invention that is neither this nor that, unnecessary and lazy. They get to think this. I use semicolons whenever it makes sense to connect two related sentences—cousin sentences. Of course you could put a period between them, but that might be a more abrupt disconnection and thus block the flow of language and meaning that you were going for.

The late, great John Gardner wrote that the fiction writer is creating a dream in the reader's mind, and the dream must be vivid and continuous. Writing is creation, not doctrine. You do have to stay within grammar, but even grammar is a little more flexible than you might think.

I tell my students they can play around with any part of speech if they can get away with it—that is, if the reader (me) does not stop and think about how the sentence should be corrected. I don't write for the anti-semicolon Church Lady crowd; I write from my heart and mind. (See how the semicolon was fine there?)

I've had the same editor for fifteen years who is very East Coast and strict grammatically, and often calls me on my hippie-dippie ways, like using "grok" or "vibe," but he never tries to get me to change semicolons to periods if they are in the natural order of things, the collagen between two complete cousinly thoughts, whose shoulders just naturally touch at the kids' table.

RULE 11:

Drop "Very" and Other Crutch Words

The word "very" seldom improves a sentence.

"VERY" WEAKENS WHAT IT MODIFIES. DELETE IT. Usually that's enough. But if, when you delete it, the remaining word is insufficient, find the appropriate substitute. The scriptwriter Tom Schulman has Robin Williams's character in *Dead Poets Society* describe this rule succinctly: "Avoid using the word 'very' because it's lazy. A man is not very tired, he is exhausted. Don't use 'very sad,' use 'morose.' Language was invented for one reason, boys—to woo women—and in that endeavor, laziness will not do." Schulman got an Oscar for lines like that.

Substitutes are easy to find:

very big—gargantuan, towering, porcine
very fast—fleet, rapid, winged, sudden

very hungry—famished, ravenous, starving
very old—ancient, hoary, antiquated

The early twentieth-century editor William Allen White reportedly told a group of reporters, "If you feel the urge of 'very' coming on, just write the word 'damn,' in the place of 'very.' The editor will strike out the word 'damn,' and you will have a good sentence."

Other crutch words that are better scrapped: "really," "some," "basically," "rather," "important." That last one, "important," loses its last remnant of power when you notice it is short for "important to *me*." If the reader can always disagree with the thing's importance, then it can't be important the way the word is meant to convey. By the way, "thing" is another of those everyday words to omit and replace with a vivid substitute.

While written language often shines at its most conversational, these oddly disempowering words have a way of troubling the reader. We readers are of two minds: We want the comfort of everyday speech and its patterns, and we want signs that the author is concisely attuned to the written idiom. In my own everyday speech I use "actually," "very," "some," "thing," and "basically" regularly, usually emphatically. My voice italicizes these weak words to make them stick.

Anne's take:

NEAL IS A STICKLER ABOUT THE USE OF "VERY," AND IN the early days of our marriage, when he edited my writing and redlined all the "verys," I used to wonder what kind of rigid, puritanical killjoy I had married. But then I did a word search in the essay I was working on and discovered I had used "very" seven times. Because he does have certain skills and charms, I decided not to pursue a legal separation, but instead to use "very" as sparingly as possible. Once you start to notice how often you are letting it in, you'll feel a mild chagrin, as if you are still in junior high and repeating "totally" every few sentences.

Maybe start experimenting with using "totes" a lot, as in, "It was totes a surprise" or "He was totes against using the word 'very.'"

Here are three sentences from the first paragraph of the introduction to *Bird by Bird*: "Our house was very quiet after dinner—unless, that is, some of my father's writer friends were over. My father was a writer, as were most of the men with whom he hung out. They were not the quietest people on earth, but they were mostly very masculine and kind."

The "verys" add nothing. Where was the copy editor?

Then, four paragraphs down, "I was very shy and strange-looking, loved reading above everything else, weighed about forty pounds at the time, and was so tense that I walked around with my shoulders up to my ears, like Richard Nixon. I saw a home movie once of a birthday party I went to in the first grade, with all these cute little boys and girls playing together like puppies, and all of a sudden I scuttled across the screen like Prufrock's crab. I was very clearly the one who was going to grow up to be a serial killer, or keep dozens and dozens of cats. Instead, I got funny."

See? Four uses of "very" in the first five paragraphs, none of which adds a thing. Do a word search when you finish your first draft and take out almost all the "verys," unless you are describing an unusually hungry caterpillar.

RULE 12:

Jettison [All Those] Tiny Words

Remove the clutter of short words (pronouns, prepositions, connectors).

IF YOU SEE A BUNCH OF LITTLE WORDS IN A SENTENCE, you can probably get rid of some [of them].

I don't have anything against auxiliary verbs and prepositions. In their place, they're essential. But I know from experience that many in a row are a tip-off to excess verbiage. In that last sentence, does "in a row" help with meaning enough to warrant slowing down the sentence? It's a question of taste. Also, if the preposition "of" is repeated in a clause, you can probably rewrite it. "The attitude of the lord of the manor repulsed her" becomes "The lord of the manor's attitude repulsed her." Also, I'm never happy seeing "in order to" as a synonym for the quite effective "to."

(Once again, the first fourteen lines of Hamlet's soliloquy are the exception.)

Having scissors in hand, eyeing where to snip, you can spotlight redundancies. "A new dawn" becomes "dawn." "Tax haven of the rich" becomes "tax haven." "Bedridden in a hospital" becomes "hospitalized."

Folksy clichés often have redundancies and extra words: "tried and true," "to and fro," "through thick and thin," "above and beyond," "ready, willing, and able."

Conversational English often adds unnecessary prepositions: "Meet up with" seldom needs "up" or "with." I don't need the "of" to throw things out the window. "As a matter of fact" becomes "In fact," or, more commonly, gets cut right out. It gets cut out. It gets cut.

Anne's take:

I USED TO BUY LITTLE PIECES OF FURNITURE FOR HOLDing books, paper, gewgaws, whenever the most recent piece of furniture I'd bought for this purpose was crammed with stuff. So I might have three cute cabinets and bookcases in one room. And I loved each of them. One day I had an epiphany: Not only were my small pieces of furniture crammed with stuff, but my rooms were crammed with small pieces of furniture. They were low to the ground and it felt like having a few of the Seven Dwarfs in each room.

Uncramming—in all realms of life—makes everything better, clearer, lighter, whether it is the breakfast nook or a long sentence.

Look at this passage from a poem by Gary Snyder that I used as an example of perfect writing in *Bird by Bird*:

Ripples on the surface of the water—
were silver salmon passing under—different
from the ripples caused by breezes

None of us can or should even try to write like Gary Snyder. But these nineteen words are breathtaking. (Read more poetry! I have urged my writing students to study poetry for forty years now.)

Now consider the sentences I wrote to introduce Snyder's poem as I reassured the class that clarity and details would emerge in their writing the same way Polaroids develop: "One of these images might show up dimly in the lower-right quadrant of the imaginary Polaroid you took; you didn't even know at first that it was part of the landscape, and here it turns out to evoke something so deep in you that you can't put your finger on it."

Right off the bat, there are three "its," positioned like ashtrays on my tiny cabinets. And I could have written "you didn't notice that it was part of the landscape," losing "at first." "Notice" implies all of a sudden—that is, at first.

What about "and here it turns out"? Better to have written "While it evokes something . . ." And if I had given this passage to Neal to edit, he would have challenged me on the cliché "you can't put your finger on it." (See Rule 19.)

The sentences you write are in flux. You go over them, trimming, revising, and auditioning words, until you arrive at the sentence you were after all along.

RULE 13:

Dress Up "This"

Pronouns are hard for readers to follow, especially "this" and "it."

ADORN THE NAKED "THIS." PLACE A NOUN AFTER IT THAT *names* it. Not "This was hard" but "This conversation was hard." Not "This was complicated" but "This process was complicated." When you focus on the unadorned "this," the pronoun often disappears altogether, replaced by the noun itself. "This wasn't the end of it" becomes "Trouble was lurking."

You might want to expand this rule to other pronouns, too. Yes, we all agree that a pronoun refers to the last preceding noun of the same number and gender. But do you want to make your reader work that out every time? Naming the noun too often can annoy the reader, but so can littering your text with pronouns to keep track of.

As a freshman in college encountering Aristotle, I was challenged by sentences like this: "Of a pair of contraries such that they have no intermediate, one or the other must needs be present in the subject in which they naturally subsist, or of which they are predicated; for it is those, as we proved, in the case of which this necessity obtains, that have no intermediate." I couldn't believe how much Aristotle depended on pronouns. Only later did I learn that as a heavily declined language, Ancient Greek's pronouns carried information that didn't depend on "the nearest proximity" rule, but on what grammatical case the original noun displayed. A case tells you whether the noun represents a location, or a subject, or an object, or a direct object, or a possession, or even a direction. It might make more sense to be pronoun-heavy in Ancient Greek or Latin or Sanskrit. We have a few declensions in English (which give us the difference between "I," "me," and "mine"), but Aristotle had twice as many. The poor translator of my Aristotle texts was stuck with English grammar, which isn't as happy to economize with pronouns.

I learned this quite recently. This rule, I mean. My writing professor friend Alexandra Youmans brought it—this rule—to my attention in 2023. Now that I know it—this rule, that is—I find it, the rule, screaming out to me daily. I see it, this rule, everywhere. But also, it's unusual, this rule, in that it, the rule, is subject to overuse.

None of these rules is set in stone. Grammar has black-and-white rules. Persuasive writing needs to be grammatical, of course, but syntax is ambivalent toward meaning, persuasion, elegance, or anything that might be called content. Once we're in the content world of semantics, choices open up to the wild. For any one writer, some rules will be more relevant than others. Some may need to be dismissed altogether. Others can be used sparingly.

Anne's take:

I'M NOT SURE WHAT I CAN ADD TO THIS, EXCEPT TO attack Neal for dredging up Aristotle. Really, Neal? When he quotes something like this at an otherwise pleasant gathering, I look away, with a dead, flat, reptilian expression, no matter that his audiences seem to enjoy the discussion.

I recommend that you ignore the quote and his ensuing remarks.

However, he is right about "this" and "it." They can be hard to follow.

Thirty-five years ago, my editor thought it made sense to make me a list of my most annoying habits as a writer. I am not making this up. I remember two, and live by them. The first was the overuse of "this" and "it," often at the beginning of a sentence. Either is a lazy way for any of us regular writers to begin, although Jane Austen begins *Pride and Prejudice* with "it." ("It is a truth universally acknowledged, that a single man in possession of a good fortune, must be in want of a wife.") As does George Orwell in *1984*. ("It was a bright cold day in April, and the clocks were striking thirteen.") Notice, though, that in both cases the subject the pronoun refers to follows right after it; the author has introduced a speck of suspense. Notice also the perfectly fine use of the verb "to be." Opening with a fixed notion of existence is a tip-off that the world is about to wobble.

Promise me you won't write the naked "this" or the isolated "it" anymore, unless you are as good a writer as Austen or Orwell or as brave a writer as Snoopy. His novels always began, "It was a dark and stormy night," but he was a dog, a beagle. (I mean no offense to you beagles.) Even "The night was dark and stormy" is an improvement.

Help us out. "This" what? "This was what she so objected to" might be "All that punning was what she so objected to" or "Her habit of scrubbing the dishes before putting them in the dishwasher was what finished the marriage." Ask yourself each time, "This" what? And which "it"? The three-legged dog, or the sandwich he snatched off an old man? The watering can or the water it held?

For the record, the second rule I remember was that I used "just" way too often: "She just had to wonder why the man wore a snorkel mask at the library" or "There was just a little more cumin in the soup than absolutely necessary" or "He was just positive that a little more cumin wouldn't hurt."

Of course, you can write any way you want, if you can get away with it—that is, keep us reading. All the people I love have, sadly, gotten much older and no longer share an enthusiasm for experimental writing. We once loved James Joyce and Gertrude Stein and Céline, who were celebrated for their avant-garde writing because they were brilliant, groundbreaking, and fearless. Now, not so much. We do not want to have to figure out what you are trying to say. I'm in it for the story. Help me see your story as you tell it. I wouldn't get to page 3 of Thomas Pynchon now.

Challenge every "this" and "it." You'll leave a lot of them in, but do better when you can. Neal asked, "Do you want to make your reader work that out every time?" Of course not. You want them to keep reading, savoring your images, voice, and clarity, grateful for a fluid ride.

RULE 14:

Remove the Boring Stuff

Spend less time defending what you've written, and more time revealing the truth.

DON'T EXPLAIN. WRITERS ARE PAID TO ARTICULATE hidden, complex, and sophisticated concepts through clever storytelling. The temptation is to prove the concept at hand, which is like showing your work in arithmetic. It's an ingrained habit. In college we trained in educational texts that featured proofs, examples, and an expectation of a logical thread that displayed all components as it progressed from cause to effect. That's the intellectual model. In fiction, authors create believable characters whose decisions create actions that drive the plot along. In nonfiction, writers describe events and arguments that pursue meaning and catharsis. The author has to know how the character made that decision or how the facts add up to a particular conclusion, including lots of backstory and logic, but the reader—or listener if, say, it's a political speech—doesn't always need all the background. Unlike in school, showing your work is not necessarily a virtue.

Most of the boring stuff that needs to be removed is excess logical detail. Yes, people go to the bathroom, but that's seldom a place for action relevant to the story, unless porcelain is the setting for an adulterous tryst during a party. Yes, that minor character wears fifties-style birdwing eyeglass frames because she's stuck in a conservative nostalgia for the past, but you can let the frames appear on her face without explanation. And if the reader misses the point, well, it's a minor character. Yes, *Brown v. Board of Education* was decided as much on modern sociological principles as on legal precedent, but unless you're writing for a legal audience, that argument is probably less relevant than you think and you can leave it out.

Sometimes explaining is necessary and right. At the end of a crime novel, a side character might ask the detective how they knew something, and that leads to a reminder of a clue the reader likely missed. But a little explaining goes a long way. Too much explaining is called "telegraphing," and it's not only boring, but insulting, too. We don't want to be told things we can figure out on our own; reading a novel is solving a puzzle, anticipating consequences, trying to stay ahead of a fast-moving plot. We tease our brains with novels. If too much is explained, we find ourselves in a paint-by-numbers art class—accurate but lifeless.

As an inveterate explainer, I'm prone to overdoing it.

Sometimes long after I've published something, I'll notice a flaw in logic, often what's called an enthymeme—jumping past a necessary condition to a conclusion. The root equation of logic is the syllogism, which has three steps: "All men are mortal. Socrates is a man. Therefore, Socrates is mortal." If I write "All men are mortal. Socrates is therefore mortal," I've left out the middle term. It's a form of jumping to conclusions, and a strict taboo in academic writing.

No reader has ever pointed out a flaw in logic to me. Either they don't care, or they don't notice. Which frees me to include only the parts of an argument or scene that might leave an impression. Let the reader assume you know what you're talking about. You're not a professor or logician when writing for the casual reader.

Hinting, foreshadowing, and misdirecting are all paths to the truth. Often, explaining isn't just unnecessary; it spoils the punch line. As puzzle solvers, we want only enough information to feel proud of getting to the answer ourselves. Too much information and we think, "Well, any jerk could have figured that out." Hints keep the game fair. Foreshadowing sets the frame for the mind. Misdirection allows for appropriate curveballs and later revelations; we want things to not quite be what they seem, especially at the beginning of a puzzle. Otherwise where's the fun?

A meaning is what comes at the end of everything we conceive or do. Part of doing and conceiving things is concluding them. We substitute the word "meaning" for the word "conclusion," but that's mostly what a meaning is: a sentence played back to oneself at the end of an experience. In that way, a meaning is the last square entered in a crossword puzzle. Once entered, the puzzle registers as complete. I never have to look at it again.

Anne's take:

OF ALL THE MOST IMPORTANT RULES, THIS IS THE MOST important one of all. I think Neal has done a good job addressing the issue, although I think the stuff about enthymeme, and Socrates, is a little boring; also, show-offy. You have to give him credit, though, for how succinctly he describes the problem and the solution. Take out about a third of the descriptions, editorializing, and details.

I assume that Neal's original meditation on this rule was somewhat longer, however, and he already did take out (most of) the boring stuff.

FYI, as I am writing nonfiction these days, I also go through the final draft and take out all the lies that I can bear to part with. I probably leave in close to a quarter of the lies, the ones that I might call exaggerations, or composites. I definitely take out the things I shoehorned in that I wish had happened but didn't, or that put me in a more sympathetic/desperate light so the reader will feel sorry for me or anxious on my behalf, and like me more. There is nothing more stunning than the truth presented as carefully and unvarnished as one can get away with; and nothing more boring than a lot of details and descriptions that make you feel like you're listening to an eight-year-old narrate a movie plot.

RULE 15:

Refresh Your Words

Don't repeat a distinctive word unless you must.

DON'T REPEAT THE SAME WORD IN A PARAGRAPH. DON'T repeat the same unusual usage in a chapter. Don't repeat the same aphorism in a book. Thought-through exceptions are frequent. (Prepositions, pronouns, connectors—those sorts of skeleton tools of speech—don't count.)

We humans seek novelty. We constantly pull things close to examine them. We call it curiosity. Or joy. They're oddly the same thing, curiosity and joy. We want to catch what's new and different, and get tickled by the knowledge or the upcoming puzzle and how the new object fits in.

If I encounter a distinctive word, I don't want to see it again for a while. I already got a kick out of it, and as with my taste buds, I need time between bites before it can again jolt me with a thrill. Keep 'em drooling.

Above, I get away with repeating the words "curiosity" and "joy" because I've offered them in a novel switch, making them synonyms.

An exception to not repeating a distinctive word is called "bridging." Sometimes using a word or phrase repeatedly helps speed the reader from one sentence to the next, in a rhythmic trance.

Here's a single stanza from Edgar Allan Poe that bridges through repeating a name:

For the moon never beams, without bringing me dreams
Of the beautiful Annabel Lee;
And the stars never rise, but I feel the bright eyes
Of the beautiful Annabel Lee;

There's a reason Martin Luther King's March on Washington Address became known as the "I Have a Dream" speech.

For ten years starting in 1966, televangelist Kathryn Kuhlman began her weekly show with the words "I believe in miracles. Why do I believe in miracles? Because I believe in God." "I believe" and "miracles" rose as sturdy bulwarks to contain her message—and her flock.

Anne's take:

YOU CANNOT USE AN EXOTIC WORD TWICE IN THE SAME book, because we will feel we have caught you trying to slip something past us, and we will turn on you. Also, never use "bloom" even though it is a beautiful word, because everyone has taken to overusing it to sound poetic. Once you start to look for "bloom," it will disrupt every work of fiction you read, and ruin otherwise pleasant literary experiences.

Only in emergency situations is it OK to use "granular," "existential," "myriad," "bespoke," "lament," and, of course, "cherish." The committee is out on "luminous." I also don't recommend any word that you pause to carefully define in your mind before setting down, such as "liminal."

This is yet another reason you need someone to look over your work before you send it off to an editor or agent in the hope of publication: Your own eye will have glanced off exotic words that you have repeated, in its desire to keep moving through the material. People have found descriptions and even one-liners repeated in my early drafts, but more frequently phrases that I just love, love, love. This is not a moral failing, but the reality of having to keep track of various ideas and characters over many pages. If a friend catches repeated or pretentious words in your manuscript before you send it off, it is customary to offer them your first grandchild or a fancy dinner, their choice.

RULE 16:

Know Your Words Inside and Out

Examining the etymology of words makes them more concrete and useful.

THE COMPLETE ETYMOLOGY OF A WORD IS TUCKED INTO its current meaning. Know your important words' origins. Most words trace back to orientation (up/down, front/back) or resources (full/empty). So does most of life; our basic functions are to go places for things to fill up our stomach or bag or time, and our most sophisticated ideas also have direction and fulfillment. Sometimes just noticing the connections to a word's antecedents can open up new passages to write. Say I'm discussing truth, which originally meant "tree." By picturing a tree, I might note solidity, permanence, aliveness, stillness, slowness, cycles, and rootedness as possible attributes of the truth I'm describing. When a word sticks out as distinctive or strange or somehow important to the text, you might investigate its etymology.

Writing is about connections and leaps of imagination, and those too are tucked into etymologies.

Three words—synonyms usually—fascinate me more than any other: "satisfaction," "equanimity," and "contentment." While most of our decisions are made from at least faint dissatisfaction, we hope to land in satisfaction. Buddhists describe equanimity as a desirable state of grace, maybe the ultimate result of all that meditation. Contented cows produce the best milk, we're told. Now where do these words come from and why do I care?

"Satisfaction" etymologically leads us to satiation, which is a property of digestion, and the opposite of hunger. What would it mean if satisfaction left me with the feeling of a hamburger in my belly? That sounds crass at first, but don't we have sexual hunger, too? Or an appetite for work or play? Something in our past recognized a kinship between food and sex, work, and play. Knowing that might lead the characters in your novel into new understandings.

"Equanimity" etymologically takes us to an ancient word for "calmness" pressed against a word for "mind" that refers further back to a synonym for "breath." So I might notice a calm breath after exercise, or during meditation, or the calm mind that allows me to stop being offended by other people's foibles.

"Contentment" is the weirdest of the three. It hearkens back to a Proto-Indo-European word for "extension," as if this kind of grace is tied to a feeling of expansiveness or limitlessness or simply space. If I'm content, does the world empty of things and smooth out into a plain? If your character is described as "content" as he is driving, do his eyes scan out to the horizon?

So three words that mean about the same thing emerge from distinct human interests that offer the possibility of liberation: breath, relief from hunger, and expansiveness. Why are these three words so interesting to me? For one thing, they're about all we have to describe the endpoint of all our yearning in one word. You'd think we'd have dozens of words that mean exactly what these three represent—one pinnacle of human experience—but we don't.

By the way, knowing that the word "truth" is derived from an ancient word for "tree" might give you the statement "as true as a tree," which oddly enough isn't a cliché. Feel free to steal it and take credit for coining a new metaphor.

Anne's take:

SOME OF YOU—A FEW OF YOU—WILL NOT END UP getting published, but that is not the point of the writing life. If you're a writer, the point is to write, at least a little every day, and to commit to full immersion in the writing life. This means reading about craft, sitting at the feet of masters from every era, studying how they create brilliance, and becoming better and better writers. Learning where words spring from enhances your fascination for what we are all up to here, which is creating meaning.

Writing? Did someone mention writing? Let's look up the roots of the word "writing." It goes back through the Middle English word *writen*, from Old English *wrītan*, from Proto-Germanic *wrītaną* ("to carve, write"), and finally from the Proto-Indo-European **wrey-* ("to rip, tear").

Do you love that? To carve. Into bark, which is what papyrus is made from, and on which people began telling their stories 4,500 years ago. To tear down, like Murasaki Shikibu in the eleventh century, Charles Darwin and Shakespeare and Harriet Beecher Stowe, Karl Marx, Walt Whitman, and Emily Dickinson.

Writing: Wow. To carve into, to tear down, to create.

The verb "to create" is from the Proto-Indo-European root **ḱerh*, whose original meaning seems to have been "to grow."

To grow! To plant, to seed, to tend to, to produce, to bring forth. This is the very work of the writer, to create a garden into which the reader may enter, with a path from where we begin, through the main characters—the commoners (daisies, poppies), the elite people (purple Eleanor Roosevelt irises, yellow roses of Texas), and the weeds, those damn weeds. And the soil, the rocks and earth you have chosen to root your stories in, with words.

My brilliant friend the writer Abigail Thomas was feeling guilt-stricken for putting together a happy life after her husband had to move permanently to a nearby nursing home: "So I got my *American Heritage Dictionary of Indo-European Roots*, looked up 'guilt,' which had historically always been 'guilt'; ugh—nothing useful there. Then I looked up 'acceptance,' and found it had derived from a word meaning 'a thread used in weaving.' My life changed on that dime."

RULE 17:

Stay In Tune

The better word is both precise and unnoticed. A thesaurus is your book of magic spells.

IF A WORD READS FALSE TO ME, IT WILL TO THE READER.

In some ways you want to underestimate your reader's intelligence. Don't use obscure words. Fill in the gaps. Dumb down while conveying the same information. But in other ways, you can't overestimate your reader's smarts. They will pick out anything that looks phony, out of place, or not quite right. Part of keeping the scenery seamless is getting the words just ducky.

Use your damn thesaurus. Yes, it's full of fancy words, but it's mostly made up of common words that you don't regularly use. And one of them is closest to what you mean. As a cub reporter at the *Daily Freeman* forty-five years ago, I would often lean across to my fellow scribe Craig Gilbert's desk and call out, "I need a word for [so-and-so]." If I said, "The owner of a clothes store," Craig would respond instantly, "Haberdasher." I resented his talent enormously.

But I also knew that "haberdasher" would look ridiculous in a daily newspaper unless used to describe Harry Truman. "No, that won't work. What else you got?" And Craig would rattle away, "Storekeeper, proprietor, merchant . . ." until he hit the right one and I cut him off with, "Retailer. That's it!" When I no longer worked in the same newsroom as Craig, I bought the fattest thesaurus I could find. Now I go online.

I also now have an Annie around. More than half of our time collaborating–reading, remarking, editing, discussing–is spent on synonyms.

She calls out from the other room, "What's the word for the plastic thingamabob at the end of a shoelace?"

"Aglet."

"Oh, dear. I'll use 'tip.'"

This commandment to find the perfect word trips over Rule 15, which suggests that you shouldn't use the same word twice in a paragraph. You lose all your points for not repeating a word when the second reference is a stretch. "The thirty-six rules were a *formula* for success. Other writing *algorithms* had failed him." Sometimes it's hard work to find the right word. It might force a change in sentence structure. My friend Yeshim Ternar used to write her short stories in longhand, and in tiny handwriting stacked possible synonyms on top of prominent words. She knew to torture the critical words. She seemed to spend as much time reviewing individual words as she did writing the sentences in the first place.

When I was newspapering, I often got into my biggest trouble with sources or subjects over an unfortunate word choice. Early in my career, I reported the discovery of the body of a missing hiker. Imagine how his parents felt when they saw my story refer to his remains as his "carcass." I found out when they complained to the publisher. A month later in a story about an amateur astronomer, I mentioned the portly gentleman's "distended stomach," and to my everlasting shame received a nasty letter in which he described a harrowing disease that swelled his abdomen, and he banned me for life from his backyard planetarium.

Anne's take:

SOMETIMES WHEN I AM HURRYING TO GET TO THE NEXT paragraph, or trying to impress the reader with my erudition, I'll use a word that is pretentious or overwrought, and I'll leave it there either as a placeholder or in the hopes that when I return to it in the edit, it will turn out to be fine. But when I get to it during the reread, I'll feel a minor sense of dread and embarrassment—"Oh my God, I don't even know what 'thaumaturgy' means!" (It's the ability of a magician to work real magic, instead of sleight of hand. Don't ever use it in a sentence. We'll snicker to ourselves that you are trying too hard.)

A thesaurus is great, not because you can find fancy

silver-dollar words that will make people think you are the literary Stephen Hawking, but rather because you can find the perfect buffalo-head nickel word, down-to-earth and trustworthy and all you need. That comfort, as in real life, is a wonderful thing.

Every writer has had the experience of having gone over an important sentence four or five times, obsessed with finding the right word. You like the image or the idea, but you keep changing your mind. You can't decide: Is a wispy palm frond feathery or feathered, plumed or plumose (which means having filaments of branches that sustain a feathery appearance)? "Plumose" is almost exactly right, but you cannot use it because it is obscure and esoteric and phony. But then you do! You go ahead with it. You send your work off to an editor, agent, or someone at a quarterly who has asked to see it, and you bolt awake at dawn filled with dread and self-loathing.

They are going to laugh at how pretentious you sound, and in fact read it out loud to nearby editors. "Listen to this! Plumose!"

Personally, I would use "feathery" to describe the leaflets of a frond. But the right word for me might not be the right word for you. For instance, there is a zero chance I would ever use the word "ducky," as Neal does above: "Part of keeping the scenery seamless is getting the words just ducky." I mentioned this to him, with perhaps a little contempt, and suggested he take it out. He said he was leaving it in, and our editor could decide. So if you have come upon "ducky," you'll know whose side our editor is on.

I would have said "getting the words right" or "choosing the right words."

No one expects this marriage to last.

RULE 18:

Find the Hidden Metaphor

Metaphors mirror humdrum experiences through elegant comparison. In the hands of an expert, they both illuminate and offer depth of field.

IN HIS DISCUSSION OF WRITING, TITLED *POETICS*, ARIStotle states, "The greatest thing by far is to be a master of metaphor. . . . It is a sign of genius, since a good metaphor implies an intuitive perception of the similarity in dissimilars."

Aristotle's is the common view, that metaphor is an authorial contrivance, an adornment that adds loftiness and cleverness to phrases that might otherwise sound crude or ordinary. In the right hands—think Bob Dylan or Emily Dickinson—metaphor cuts to the quick of meaning and leaves the reader a little breathless.

But our basic vocabulary, our ordinary and familiar everyday words, are also metaphorical. (I'm using the broad sense of metaphor, which includes simile and analogy.) Look at the subhead for this rule. The verb "mirror" is a metaphor; no one's literally holding up a shiny hand mirror to my page, hoping to catch sight of a metaphor. The hum in "humdrum" is from a beehive, which also shares the drone that humdrum implies. "Elegant" sounds awfully abstract, until its etymology is noticed: to pluck or root out. "In the hands of" isn't literal; an expert writer isn't showing me her palms full of goodies. She isn't hand-ing me anything. An "expert" is from the word for "first in line."

You may be tempted to insert metaphors in the most likely places—a description of an emotional reaction or a bit of local color. Go ahead and do that, making sure the metaphor captures the thought well and succinctly, pinning down a subtle characteristic of the person or experience at hand.

But metaphors fit in everywhere. A parable is a metaphor, as are allegories and analogies. Fairy tales are metaphors, as is any moral tale. Your moral thoughts operate metaphorically, taking a skeletal system of good versus bad, right versus wrong, first learned by rote as a child, then imposing it on a new situation, searching for what is similar. We call that pattern recognition. We might also call it metaphorical thinking.

Once you recognize that everything's a metaphor, your notions of how to convey information may change. Maybe you don't need a three-word metaphor; maybe what's called for is a diversion into a little story, a homespun parable, a story-within-a-story, a character's jogged memory, or an apparent non sequitur that eventually reveals a similar truth.

Annie thinks in delightful metaphors that fill her books. Here's a typical nonfiction passage where she displays that genius that Aristotle talks about: "As I drove along, I kept sniffing the air like a Doberman pinscher, until even the inside of my *nose* started to smell bad: it smelled like two tiny windowless hallways." Me? I bend to the literal; metaphors don't spring up naturally. But I try to make up for it with strong verbs ("bend to," "spring up") that hide their own metaphors.

Anne's take:

I LOVE BEAUTIFUL METAPHORS. LIFE REALLY IS A STAGE, A highway, a river, and in the right hands these basic images can do what metaphors are paid to do: explain the unknown in terms of the known. A bad metaphor is, for example, the bumpy road, although you can use those words if you are describing an actual bumpy road beneath your feet or tires. A great road metaphor can be found in songs by Bruce Springsteen and the Beatles, such as the ride along "Thunder Road," or the long and winding one. Metaphor megastar Emily Dickinson wrote, "Dying is a wild Night and a new Road." Such dark beauty and comfort!

And rivers. Maybe moon rivers, wide rivers, or many,

many of them to cross. Try out a metaphor about the river of life, its ebbs, shoals, dangers, beauty. Then try again. Don't try too hard, though, or we will notice and roll our eyes. Bad metaphors stick out like—well, I would say like sore thumbs, if Neal would not cross this out and send it back for me to try again.

Bad metaphors stick out of otherwise good sentences and songs. Let's look at the two worst metaphors in all of musical history since those first stone flutes. Number one is, of course, in "MacArthur Park," and the cake that someone left out in the rain. The writer, Jimmy Webb, whose other songs show he knows better, was describing how he felt after the catastrophic end of a passionate affair, using images he had seen in Los Angeles's MacArthur Park. Some of these visual images are lovely, such as the old men playing checkers by the trees. And then that goddamn cake. I do believe he saw such a thing and knew how this sodden cake felt, and it pierced him, but I ask you: Is this image not better to take to one's therapist, rather than include in a song of heartbreak, which will go on to be mocked for nearly five decades so far, and counting?

The runner-up in my tiny tense opinion is "A Horse with No Name." The song, by America, is about wanting to ride through a desert away from it all, the distractions, materialism, and noisy bullshit of life in the city. The narrator claims to be on a horse with no name. This is worrisome to the listener: The man can be searching without destination, just going with the flow, but there is no rideable horse without a name on earth. How does the cowboy get said horse's attention, to giddyup, or trot on? Did he shout, "Hey, you with the big butt!" or use a clicker? Trust me, the horse had a name. The metaphor comes off as contrived, and therefore meaningless.

If your metaphor is forced, take it out. I have a couple of editors on almost everything I write, first Neal and then the book or magazine editor, and believe me, they seize upon forced metaphors. They save me from myself.

Try each metaphor out carefully, and see it if feels natural. Does it add depth and meaning, or conversely, an exciting kind of mystery? Neal's little friend Plato wrote, "Time is the moving image of eternity." I mean—whoa, dude!

(By the way, while we're on the subject of metaphors, my father described Beethoven's Fifth Symphony as metaphor upon metaphor. Duh duh duh *duh*. Duh duh duh *duh*: Life is pounding on the door and then barges in with all the joy and hardship, darkness and light, life and death and new life.)

Over and over, every rule of Neal's is about creating better sentences, cleaner and richer at the same time. A successful metaphor—"love is a rose bush, beautiful and prickly and ephemeral"—enhances its environment, as does taking out a forced one.

RULE 19:

Twist Clichés

We already think in clichés; you owe it to your reader's search for novelty to remove or deconstruct your hackneyed phrases.

USE CLICHÉS TO YOUR HEART'S DESIRE, BUT ONLY IF YOU twist them until they bleed. We're pattern seekers, us humans, and that means that our ideas—our spoken words—rest on hackneyed ideas that are recombined in new ways. Clichés 'R' us. We're spitting out old thoughts all day long. Writers think like everyone else. We have an alphabet, and we also have a canon of idiomatic shortcuts to abstract ideas—adages and stale phrases. (So do musicians. How many times have you heard a jazz soloist blurt out a phrase from a childhood ditty?)

Don't be scared to write the first thing that comes into your head, which is often a cliché. Later you can exchange it for all-new verbiage. But you might also use the cliché as a starting point and create a zinger out of it, like a comedian taking a mundane experience and throwing in an unexpected variable, getting a laugh.

I might first think, "She was good as gold." By the time I've finished creating the character, the line has changed to "She was good as brass, barely."

A year or so into my newspaper career I was assigned the storm story. Writing about snowstorms in upstate New York is like writing about waves in Waikiki Beach or pit crews at Talladega. But a good-sized blizzard, no matter how much it resembles every other good-sized blizzard, must be placed on the front page. Every reader expects it; the storm is what everyone is talking about, so it must be news. What can you possibly say that is fresh enough to do more than convey the same facts that appear on the weather page deep inside the paper?

I still remember my lede:

"Cold, cold, cold. Freezing. It was freezing." Now, I knew why I wrote those words, even if my readers didn't. They were the first words of a song by the band Little Feat. (A paraphrase, really. The original repeats "Cold, cold, cold"—six "colds"—before adding "Freezing.") My editor and I both knew that the allusion would be lost on all but a handful of our readers, but so what? It was a weather story, and anything other than a cliché was an improvement. This event stuck in my mind—the ridiculousness of my lede, as well as its necessity—and it was on that day that I realized much of my job as a newspaper writer was to reject the clichés. I stopped being a newspaper writer more than thirty years ago. I still find myself deleting or twisting first-thought clichés every time I write. "So it goes" becomes "So it stops." "You take the good with the bad" becomes "You take the mediocre with the bad." Ian Fleming turned "live and let live" into "Live and Let Die."

Anne's take:

WELL, SURE, MOSTLY. EVERY SO OFTEN, HOWEVER, YOU simply need to use one of the lesser-known clichés, because there are only so many words and phrases in the English language.

Let me give you an example: I googled a list of clichés, and under the *A*s, there were 213 so-called clichés. 213! Here are four side-by-side clichés that begin with the letter *A*:

as happy as a clam
as happy as a sandboy
as happy as Larry
as honest as the day is long

Now, obviously you cannot use "happy as a clam," only partly because clams are not happy creatures. They are cold and have sand in some very special places, and you know exactly how miserable that can be. Also, we are going to try and catch them, and kill them so we can eat them. So maybe you could say, "miserable as a clam." But this brings us to "sandboy," a young peddler of sand who sold it to barkeepers to absorb spills and spit on the floor. Sandboys were happy because they got paid for the delivery, but also they could sweep up the old sand before spreading the new and maybe find some loose change. Even happier! But who among you knew that? Probably only Neal, and his ilk. So I am going to recommend you use the phrase "happy as a sandboy" in whatever you are currently working on.

This brings us to Larry. "As happy as Larry." Is Larry a clam? Probably not, yet according to Neal, I am still instructed not to use the phrase, which I've never heard or read. Maybe it bears investigating just why Larry is so happy—or is he only pretending to be happy? Don't you want to know more about Larry? You could investigate the way you might any fictional character: What does he look like, and how do clothes hang on him, and does his voice change when he is worried? What does he do with his hands when he is bored or in an intimate conversation? I say hats off to Larry.

And I'm definitely not going to say he is as honest as the day is long, because it's criminally overused. It has been a criminally overused cliché for centuries. But if you follow Neal's advice to twist it, you could use "as honest as a clam," because clams don't have the bandwidth to lie. Or you could say, "as honest as the day was long, when that used to mean something, in the old days before the insane speed of this modern life, when days race by like rabbits." Or you could say he was truthful, full of truth.

I do encourage you to use clichés in first drafts as a space holder so that you don't bog down and lose momentum. You can return to them later and see if you can come up with something more original and interesting. The most important thing I can share is to do whatever it takes to avoid coming to a standstill while your inner critic tries to convince you to give up. Is "Never give up" a cliché? My son has it tattooed on his forearm, but whether it is or not, don't. Don't ever give up on writing.

RULE 20:

Knock Three Times

For a series of terms to land, you usually need three.

IN ENGLISH, THREE IS THE MAGIC NUMBER. *THE GOOD, the Bad, and the Ugly. The Lion, the Witch, and the Wardrobe. I, Me, Mine.* Years ago, my bilingual Turkish and English writer friend Yeshim Ternar told me that when she switched into English she had to remember that two examples of anything, which are enough in Turkish, are insufficient to her American audience. It's more about the rhythm than the words, actually. Think of the musical pattern "duh-dah duh-dah" and how unresolved it sounds compared to "duh-dah duh-dah duh-dah." It's hard to sing the longer version without adding a big, resolving accent to the last "dah." We read lists—especially lists of three—rhythmically.

The rule of threes emerges naturally when you read your words aloud. When you follow the instruction to read back your work before submitting it to an editor, you'll hear your own mistakes—and mostly we're talking about mistakes of rhythm. Like poetry, prose relies on rhythm; it's just not necessarily metrical. Call it conversational rhythm. We like our pauses, our punch lines, our crescendos, and our familiar patterns. Three examples is a familiar pattern. Two things can be alike in many ways. Three things can be alike in few ways.

All that said, as Annie points out below, two examples without the third have their own rhythm, which might better fit your work in progress. Rules of grammar are black-and-white and give you a simple choice of right or wrong. Rules of rhetoric or persuasion are subtle and yielding. When collaborating with another, or even yourself, recognize that everybody's voice has its quirks. Early on in our relationship, I was jarred by Annie's use of twos rather than threes. But I knew better than to correct it. Her voice, her choice. Eventually, I could recognize the power of her dangling twos.

Anne's take:

THIS RULE OF THREES IS TRUE FOR NEAL AND PROBABLY most writers. I use two in a series as often as I do three. It's what I'm comfortable with, and what sometimes works best for my rhythm, emphasis, or humor.

I notice perfect twos everywhere. And here is a stunning two inside a series of four that I came upon years ago in a description of Robert Campin's painting *Portrait of a Woman*. "I don't know what I love more: the eyes, the subtlety of the purple robe, the incredible headscarf (the layers! the folds!) or the pins."

"The layers! The folds!" If you google the painting, you'll see what I mean about this description's greatness. The quote is from Campin's star pupil, Peter Paul Rubens.

My subject matter—family, soul, spirit, humanity, and coming through hard times—allows for a lot of open-ended thoughts without simple resolution, which threes don't. Three in a series would leave my words wrapped up in neat, tight packages, which is the opposite of what I'm trying for. Two in a series adds suspense, as I haven't closed off the thought process.

Either is fine. Don't let Neal tell you otherwise. Try things one way, move them around, take stuff out, and see if more spaciousness is what you were after. If two is too abrupt, try three, unless you don't have a third example. Picasso said, "If I don't have red, I use blue." See what works.

RULE 21:

Stretch Out

Long sentences require attention to detail, conjunctions, and rhythm—and a payoff at the end.

LONG SENTENCES ARE ACCEPTABLE, BUT THEY NEED TO BE linear, propulsive, and forward-moving, with parentheticals that don't double back. Used judiciously, a long sentence catapults the reader through real time with urgency, immediacy, and a sense of working consciousness.

Here's a 280-word sentence from Nikolai Gogol's "The Overcoat":

> Even at the hour when the grey St. Petersburg sky had quite dispersed, and all the official world had eaten or dined, each as he could, in accordance with the salary he received and his own fancy; when all were resting from the departmental jar of pens, running to and fro from their own and other people's indispensable occupations, and from all the work that an uneasy man makes willingly for himself, rather than what is

> necessary; when officials hasten to dedicate to pleasure the time which is left to them, one bolder than the rest going to the theatre; another, into the street looking under all the bonnets; another wasting his evening in compliments to some pretty girl, the star of a small official circle; another—and this is the common case of all—visiting his comrades on the fourth or third floor, in two small rooms with an anteroom or kitchen, and some pretensions to fashion, such as a lamp or some other trifle which has cost many a sacrifice of dinner or pleasure trip; in a word, at the hour when all officials disperse among the contracted quarters of their friends, to play whist, as they sip their tea from glasses with a kopek's worth of sugar, smoke long pipes, relate at times some bits of gossip which a Russian man can never, under any circumstances, refrain from, and, when there is nothing else to talk of, repeat eternal anecdotes about the commandant to whom they had sent word that the tails of the horses on the Falconet Monument had been cut off, when all strive to divert themselves, Akakiy Akakievitch indulged in no kind of diversion.

Whatever you think of the sentence, it's mostly staccato, never gets hung up on metaphysics, doesn't double back even when relying on memory, contains few Latinate multisyllabic words, slows down only to catch a breath and then resumes its urgency, and feels possible as a true stream of consciousness as well as a complete picture of the dreary lives of bureaucrats, both at the office and in their attempt to enliven themselves in the dark, ultimately rewarding the reader with a whammy of a punch line.

What you just read—my quick characterization of the sentence's style—is also an acceptable long sentence. Don't fear long sentences, and don't fear the comma as a substitute for the period. Sometimes the long sentence is not an enemy.

Anne's take:

MANY OF OUR GREATEST WRITERS HAVE USED LONG, LONG SENTENCES, such as James Joyce and William Faulkner, but it has been decades since I felt like reading them. There is a nearly 4,400-word stream-of-consciousness passage in Joyce's *Ulysses*, not so much a sentence as an outburst, which I think is very nice and which thrilled me in high school when I first read the book, but somewhat less so in my early twenties when I ostentatiously reread the book so that people would think I am smarter than I am.

My reading group chose *Ulysses* when I was thirty, and by this point I mostly found it impenetrable. I had to pretend to have read the 150 pages we were supposed to consume every two weeks. Anything I contributed had been cribbed from various forewords and introductions I read at the library. When I contributed my stolen bons mots, I made sure to stroke my chin like William Buckley.

If you are an excellent writer, go ahead and experiment with 100-word sentences. Margaret Atwood, Vladimir Nabokov, and Virginia Woolf sometimes use long sentences, and I love nearly every word they have written, but most of the time I find long, long sentences difficult to track, and annoying. The rule, though, is that you can get away with anything in your writing as long as your reader wants to keep reading and not run away screaming. Of course, Faulkner could get away with sentences that were a thousand words because of the greatness of the writing. An extremely long Faulkner sentence is stunning and brilliant, worthy of awe. But please raise your hand if you have been reading a lot of Faulkner since Covid. Neal, put your hand down.

While I have you, here is the most perfect 107-word sentence in the English language, from *Stuart Little* by E. B. White. It takes place near the end, when Stuart is searching for Margalo in Ames Crossing. If you are going to use long sentences, try to write more like this:

> In the loveliest town of all, where the houses were white and high and the elm trees were green and higher than the houses, where the front yards were wide and pleasant and the back yards were bushy and worth finding out about, where the streets sloped down to the stream and the stream flowed quietly under the bridge, where the lawns ended in orchards

and the orchards ended in fields and the fields ended in pastures and the pastures climbed the hill and disappeared over the top toward the wonderful wide sky, in this loveliest of all towns Stuart stopped to get a drink of sarsaparilla.

RULE 22:

Short Sells

Interrupt lyrical or otherwise long passages with an abrupt, short sentence.

SHORT ALSO WORKS. USE INTENTIONALLY SHORT SENtences to bring the reader home. Like this.

Famously, this admonition was the first of Ernest Hemingway's four rules for writing: "Use short sentences. Use short first paragraphs. Use vigorous English. Be positive, not negative." All good rules (and all short sentences). Of course, he wanted all sentences to be short. If you want to sound like Hemingway, do so. But I'm encouraging you to use short sentences occasionally, as punctuation. One of my favorite books is *The Old Man and the Sea*. But I'm equally wowed by *Absalom, Absalom!* and Faulkner's notoriously long sentences. That book contains what once held the record for "longest legitimate published sentence in the English language," a thought-out, fast-paced, and fully cogent spill of 1,288 words. Faulkner was no stream-of-consciousness writer, but he excelled at baring his characters' thoughts.

By the way, here is the paragraph that precedes that longest sentence:

> "Yes," Quentin said.

And what sentence *follows* the longest sentence?

> "Yes," Quentin said.

Same short, punctuating sentence.

Like I said, occasional short sentences. For dramatic effect.

The punch line doesn't have to be a short sentence; it might be a clause that manages to stand alone at the end of a sentence. Look at how this Hank Williams verse concludes:

The silence of a falling star
Lights up a purple sky
And as I wonder where you are
I'm so lonesome, I could cry

"I could cry." There's nothing more final than that. Lyricists have it over book writers in expressing the obvious without irony or fancification.

Anne's take:

THE TWO MOST PROFOUND SENTENCES I'VE EVER READ are both only two words. One is the description of Dilsey, the black matriarch of the Compton family servants in *The Sound and the Fury*:

"Dilsey endured."

Her family came through their hideous racist treatment and station in life, but because of Dilsey's faith, goodness, and dignity, her love of all of God's creation, they endured.

The other is the shortest sentence in the Bible:

"Jesus wept."

In the gospel of John, Jesus finally arrives in Bethany after being sent for by Mary and Martha, whose brother Lazarus—Jesus's dear friend—is very sick. By the time Jesus arrives, perhaps a bit lackadaisically, Lazarus has been dead for four days. He lies in a cave, wrapped in burial clothing. Jesus wept. We know firsthand what those two words mean—his extreme grief at the death of his friend. But this being the Bible, we can assume he is weeping for all of humanity, the terrible pain we must all experience because our most beloved people die. And, at the same time, in these two words, we remember that Jesus is a man, a human, born of a mother, with bodily fluids—tears!

Needless to say, none of us can write like Faulkner or John, but I think Neal is right when he urges short sentences on you, to stop the reader, make them take in the profundity we come upon in life. If your efforts feel pretentious, don't give up. Here are the most important words a writer can take to heart:

Try again.

And I can't let this opportunity pass without reminding you of what Calvin Coolidge said to a reporter who told him a friend had bet him that he couldn't get more than two words out of the president:

"You lose."

RULE 23:

Give Your Sentence a Finale

Even if you begin your sentence with a punch, end it stronger.

THE STRONGEST ELEMENT OF A SENTENCE USUALLY belongs at the end. That strength is often punchy. It's short and sweet or terse and abrupt. "My brother got the hiccups on the way to the movies" versus "On the way to the movies, my brother got the hiccups."

The strongest element isn't necessarily the loudest; it can be something unusual or unexpected or gripping.

Think of a sentence as a line of poetry. So much rides on the last word or syllable of a line of poetry: That final word is usually followed by a pause, as a sentence is by a period. The last word hangs around for a little longer. In its luxurious pause will it echo, mirror, complement, disturb, entice, suspend? Since a verb is often the most powerful and important word in the sentence, it can work well to push the verb as close to the period as possible. Rather than writing "We smashed through the guardrail and sailed over the cliff in our 1997 Honda Civic with the faulty brakes," you could try "Our 1997 Honda Civic with the faulty brakes smashed through the guardrail, and over the cliff we sailed."

Sometimes it's right to back into the sentence, leaving the subject and verb to the end, for effect: "With his face dark in shadow from the bunched pin oak leaves overhead, only the whites of his eyes showed."

If the end of the sentence can't manage to be the strongest, then backtrack to the beginning. That's second best. For instance: "Bullets sprayed around his head, but none found skin."

Anne's take:

ALL I CAN ADD TO THIS IS THAT AS A READER, THERE IS almost no greater experience than when a sentence sticks the landing, and you look up and savor that literary moment in time. One of the most famous last lines in American literature is Fitzgerald's in *The Great Gatsby*: "So we beat on, boats against the current, borne back ceaselessly into the past."

That's as perfect as it gets, but you and I are probably not going to come up with that level of greatness. What we can do is create clean, honest sentences that glide to completion.

Let me give you an example. Here is a recent rough paragraph:

> So I managed to figure out how to get free of the algae and crawl out of the chilly lake by first finding something solid on the bank that was a little mucky, then hoisting myself out by first grabbing a clump of grasses that miraculously held, and pulling myself up.

My job is to take out all the excess. Now it reads:

> I figured out how to get free of the algae in the chilly lake and hoist myself out, by first grabbing hold of something on the bank that was solid but mucky. It was too slippery. I then grabbed a clump of grass, held tight, and pulled myself up.

The most dynamic aspects of those sentences are the hoisting, and the good news that the clump of grasses held. The paragraph now becomes:

> I kicked free of the algae in the chilly lake and grabbed something solid and mucky on the bank. My hand slipped. I grasped a clump of grass and pulled. It held. And I hoisted my spent body.

OK, it's not Mary Oliver or Thoreau, but we can see it

now and feel some energy. Move the words of your sentence like puzzle pieces.

Sometimes I'll come up with a sentence at the end of a paragraph that pulls this off—flows naturally along like a stream, building strength and coming to rest on nice, clean words that create a still pool, and I'll know that this is exactly where the piece must end.

RULE 24:

Crystallize Your Dialogue

Dialogue needs to be as zippy and economical as the rest of the book.

DIALOGUE EXPOSES HOW CHARACTERS MAKE CHOICES, and only in passing describes their personalities. Don't let your people meander. Dialogue is crystallized thinking. Just as you don't need to show your characters excusing themselves to the bathroom, you don't need to fill the pages with hellos, goodbyes, and gossipy chatter. (Unless your character is an annoying gossip, but even then, the drivel has to be punctuated with clues to upcoming consequences.)

Pay close attention to the start of any conversation. If one character is more circumspect or withdrawn, they might not ever speak first. A garrulous character opens with a joke, not a wise comment. A physical, nonthinking character might grunt approval rather than vocalize a "yes." As much as in their actions, characters deserve consistency in their diction and interjections. The same is true for their interior dialogue.

Too little dialogue, and the reader wonders what the characters sound like, and why they're mute. Stories with little overt dialogue tend to depend on an offsetting amount of interior dialogue. Too much dialogue, and your reader begs for some action or color to relieve them from all the frustrating arguments.

This holds true in nonfiction as well. The dialogue may not be literal, in quotes, but as we readers make our way through recorded experiences, we expect to see living human beings react and interact, with thoughts and emotions. We humans participate in a well-known pattern that is repeated in virtually every fictional scene and nonfictional anecdote: situation, complication, resolution. This simple arc is expressed in other ways: desire, obstacle, solution; or thesis, antithesis, synthesis; or meeting, conflict, harmony. Some personalities just don't get along; others need an outside variable to force a conflict. But the whole point is the conflict, and that requires characters who clash. Dialogue is a quick way to watch the disagreement unfold, while revealing personalities at work. In nonfiction, the anecdote might have to replace dialogue with more inferential details: physical reactions, interior dialogue reactions. ("Allen shivered nervously on the couch as Lamott paused to clean her glasses before resuming her interest in his manuscript.")

Anne's take:

THE POINT ABOUT DIALOGUE IS THAT WE SHOULD know who is speaking by what they say—their words and rhythms. Dialogue is fraught with the potential to turn off the reader with too much explanation or repartee. (You can have either a character who speaks whimsically, or me as a reader.)

The best way to check a passage of dialogue for authenticity and ease is to read it into a recording device and play it back. Every flat or stilted note will make you cringe, but now you have a chance to get it right before giving it to someone to read and dismiss you as a fraud. Do it better. Then read it again into the recorder.

The characters know how they would talk, what they sound like, and why they need to say what they're saying. If you make them flashy, clipped, authoritative, ironic, or whatever when they aren't, those snippets of dialogue will ring false and we will not keep reading.

Some people and characters are easier to typecast memorably. I have a friend in her late thirties who speaks like a teenager. She begins most sentences, with "Well," but she says it lazily, one might say stupidly, as "Wool."

"Hey, how are you doing?"

"Wool, actually, pretty well."

"Will you stay in the Bay Area?"

"Wool, I'm thinking of moving to Portland." So she

would be easy to capture. I also have the frankly friend—"Frankly, I'm thinking of moving to Portland"—the "literally" friend, and the Harold Pinter–play friend, with his pauses and cryptic silences.

Most conversations in my life, however, are between people who sound like me, for all intents and purposes. So how would I distinguish them in a patch of dialogue? Bear down on their ages, cultures, subcultures, education, and personalities. Is the speaker earnest, sarcastic, paying attention, shy, arrogant, prone to pontificating? Hand each one a microphone and let them speak into it, and listen for what sets their speech apart.

My advice is to read the masters and see how they do it. J. D. Salinger, Raymond Carver, and Virginia Woolf are some of my favorites. Watch great modern movies whose screenwriters are legendarily great with dialogue, like Aaron Sorkin, Diablo Cody, Billy Wilder, John Sayles, Nora Ephron, William Goldman. Study how their conversations canter along without sounding clipped and arch. Then do that!

RULE 25:

In Fiction, Archetype Your Characters

Below the human stereotypes are common psychological patterns that readers expect.

DISTINGUISH YOUR CHARACTERS' PERSONALITY TYPES so they don't blur into one another. In one way, every character you write is an aspect of yourself that is worthy of exploring. But the characters themselves have to be distinct, even memorable, and consistent with the everyday conformity of personality types.

In my first draft, a character emerges as a rough-cast amalgam. As I work through the drafts, impurities are removed and the surface is burnished. I've cleaned up the exterior to make way for the interior. The comedian Duncan Trussell says that when you first meet him, you're greeting his bodyguard. That's the external view of the personality, which tends to enter the world defensively, as if in imminent danger. By the third draft, though, I'm more concerned with exposing the quirks of the character's hidden interior, the part of him that is inevitably lovely and kind and generous, even if he looks and acts like a monster. In that second-draft characterization, the lines between show and tell blur, and with confidence I can introduce contradictions.

If you're having trouble getting a precise fix on a character, Jungian archetype systems (Myers-Briggs, enneagram) are a handy guide. The Jungian charts help you sort out the character's hidden fears and yearnings (one type might be seeking love, another seeking admiration), their pet peeves, unhealthy behaviors, demanding beliefs, ability to get along with other specific personality types, perfectionism or sloppiness, concern for outward appearance, and on and on. So if your character has a chip on her shoulder, you might notice that she generally withdraws from conflict, dislikes loud noises and people, and when healthy can share unusual psychological insights. But a boastful character thrives in conflict, listens to heavy metal, and when healthy enjoys a hearty laugh over a silly subject.

Your reader is unconsciously aware of these behavioral attributes and will be annoyed if your characters don't play out their archetypal roles.

Some authors present us with archetypal characters who adorn fabulous settings and plots. Genre fiction—historical, sci-fi, horror, whatever—focuses mostly on how the characters deal with the outside world of things and other people, and their characters don't necessarily grow or change;

they're just tortured over and over again. I can name some excellent authors who write this way, but they might feel insulted. That's because we're told that characters are supposed to develop.

Writers whose characters change over time stay within the archetype model but move the character from a healthy place to an unhealthy place or vice versa. These writers often include interior dialogue, so we can have what the movies call reaction shots—a bit of a riff on how the character is thinking about the events around her. It gets quite complicated when you notice that each archetype has its own way of getting better and worse, and your reader knows intuitively when you've got that wrong.

It may take only a sentence or two to distinguish a character's external specialness—their unique set of physical attributes. Their internal specialness must be attended to through every scene they inhabit. When an actor asks "What's the motivation?" for their role's action or statement, they're tying together a coherent personality. Your characters deserve believable, complex, contradictory, and surprising personalities, like your own.

Anne's take:

EACH OF OUR CHARACTERS IS PROBABLY SOME ASPECT OF our own multilayered nature—the helper, the martyr, the know-it-all, the diplomat, etc. So it's possible to do the deep dive with each of these inner characters, who make up you, and get to know them at the level of personal inquiry. Why do you need to be right? Where does that victimized self-righteousness spring from? Why do you try to be diplomatic with a jerk?

When I wrote my second novel, *Rosie*, the little girl who had lost her father was me, although I was twenty years older. But boy, did I know the grief and emptiness and disbelief Rosie felt. Her mother, Elizabeth, was an elegant alcoholic, and while I was not elegant, I could write the hell out of her alcoholism. Elizabeth's best friend, a zaftig codependent with a huge heart and capacity to express love? Moi moi moi. And James, Elizabeth's future husband, was a funny writer who (like most writers) had equal proportions of grandiosity and shaky self-esteem.

The marvelous travel and spiritual writer Pico Iyer wrote, "Writing is, in the end, that oddest of anomalies: an intimate letter to a stranger." This does not mean you need to tell us your weight or the name of the person you hate most in the world and will never forgive. This means you write from who and where you are, not from who and where you think we want you to be. As the saying goes, you be you. Gaddis got to be Gaddis, Kerouac got to be Kerouac, but I have not felt moved to read either in forty years. You, on the other hand, may very well catch my attention and lure me into reading what *you* make of it all.

RULE 26:

Show, Then Tell

Start with the concrete—what happened—and after, when appropriate, riff on your thoughts about consequences.

DISASTROUSLY, YOU PROBABLY LEARNED THIS DIRECTIVE as "show, don't tell," which is often flat-out wrong and has led to a lot of strangely thin short stories populating literary journals. The central idea behind "show, don't tell" is that setting, character, voice, and plot should go a long way in satisfying the reader's curiosity. It's a helpful old rule so far as it goes: Showing things physically and through the subtlety of diction and psychological tropes is the starting point of any scene. These touchstones are necessary for the seamless world that we cherish finding.

I think of *The Great Gatsby* as the preeminent "show, don't tell" novel, and it works sublimely. Using an inconsequential, disinterested character as his narrator, Fitzgerald adopts a nonjudgmental tone throughout. Until the very end of the book, that is, when out of the blue comes this sentence:

> They were careless people, Tom and Daisy—they smashed up things and creatures and then retreated back into their money or their vast carelessness or whatever it was that kept them together, and let other people clean up the mess they had made.

It's a remarkable and memorable sentence for other reasons, but mainly it just plain sticks out. Wow. Running into it as I finish up *Gatsby*, I might mumble, "I kind of thought that about Tom and Daisy, but nobody told me to before. Now I know." All of a sudden the book is a moral tale, a tragedy, and the character Gatsby is even more sympathetic. By suddenly telling, Fitzgerald rounds out the reader's thoughts just as the tale comes to a conclusion. Fitzgerald couldn't help himself, and needed it understood that his view wasn't solipsistic, amoral, or tolerant. He wasn't modern, in other words. And he made that clear by showing and then, briefly, telling. Strangely, a couple of generations later, his progeny—the brat novelists of the eighties and nineties, for instance—pursued random landscapes of characters who are solipsistic, amoral, and tolerant. And flat. They took showing without telling to an absurd meaninglessness.

Of course most authors don't wait until the end to pass judgment or comment on their characters. They show, then tell. You get a little scenery and dialogue, then a little commentary. I think of it as showing, then riffing.

In *Absalom, Absalom!* Faulkner has Quentin say "Yes," and then for three pages we have a stream-of-consciousness riff that doesn't advance the story one instant, but tells us a lot about how Quentin sees the world.

Here's a more straightforward example. I literally pulled the first novel I saw from my shelves, *Conjugating Hindi* by Ishmael Reed.

> He sat down at the table. He tried to get back to his online Hindi lessons. It was hard to get his head wrapped around the use of prepositions in Hindi. In fact, they were post-positions. He was getting more out of Hindu history and literature than from the Hindi language, which for him was like a UFC fighter that had brought him to the mat and held him in a guillotine hold. Puttbutt said that he quit Japanese lessons when it was required that he study Kanji, which is to English what "Jaws" was to swimmers. Boa lived in the country where most of the Black intellectual fire power was taken up with convincing millions of Whites that Blacks weren't chimps, monkeys, gorillas, and apes, which was how the ancestors of these Whites were treated in Europe where they weren't considered White. The response to these literary sermons was denial and ridicule. The back and forth had become a big marketing enterprise. Moreover, men who would never be profiled racially dominated the discussion of race and when it became the version of someone who knew the experience from the inside and someone who peeped

> from behind the curtains, their version prevailed. But Chappie was right. No matter how difficult it was to train your brain to accept a new word order, the experience was worthwhile.

And it goes on, this riff. The action is at the beginning: sitting down, working out Hindi prepositions. That takes almost no time to read. But through "telling, not showing," we're taken through some thoughts about history and language and by association to racism in American literary criticism, then police profiling and the white-dominated media, and suddenly back full circle to translating Hindi, but now with a racially oriented viewpoint.

This passage isn't stream-of-consciousness meandering, but an accurate depiction of how our minds riff, collecting new variables and information on the way, culminating in newfound thoughts. Without riffing on abstractions, the plot would be pointless in a way. *Conjugating Hindi* is a book about culture and racism and history and critical theory, and also a little about someone learning a new language.

No question, a lot of the time, "show, don't tell" works. Annie Dillard instructs us not to describe emotions, implying that readers can't be compelled to feel anything just by being told how the writer or a character feels. Most feelings can be portrayed through observable behaviors. Apologies to Annie Dillard, but I'll make up an example:

> You would have thought them early birds, these few

> spectators sprinkled around the aluminum bleachers as if in their customary seats for a high school football game, this pair hunched under a blanket hiding their faces, that couple nearly back to back, the man's vision fixed on the metal foot plank where his feet splayed, the woman's red eyes facing forward, still trying to make sense of the twisted metal scaffold where the booster rocket failed, while a soldier in green fatigues on the viewing stand's top step marched head high back and forth, back and forth, an hour now since the disaster.
>
> Nowhere does it say, "They were shocked."

Anne's take:

I AM COMPLETELY FINE WITH AN AUTHOR TELLING ME useful information about the characters and their predicaments if it helps the story. Chekhov famously said, "Don't tell me the moon is shining; show me the glint of light on broken glass," and of course that is lovely, but not necessary. I'm glad to know whatever you want to tell me about the moon, whether it was full or new, yellow or white, bright or behind clouds, or that today, an unmanned American spacecraft landed on it—you don't need to show me a close-up of the American flag. Tell me.

Tell me when you can save me a lot of time before getting

to an important moment in the paragraph or plot. Tell me to spare me from tedium. Tell me to skip having to repeat yourself.

"This was Ed Shap's first girlfriend and he was drenched in flop sweat." We see the spreading wetness.

"Ed had thrown up his lunch an hour before but had brushed his teeth since." Poor Ed. Good information and we didn't have to watch.

"Now his breath smelled faintly of minty soup." We know a lot in three sentences—how vulnerable he is, how much he cares that all goes well. I for one feel that he is going to get through this date without losing his first girlfriend on a technicality.

As always, the rule is that you can do anything in your writing that works, that you can get away with, that is satisfying to the reader.

RULE 27:

Give Them a Hero's Welcome

Start off by telling the reader who to root for.

IF YOU'RE WRITING FICTION, WITHIN A PAGE OR SO OF your protagonist appearing, prove through the eyes of another character that they are lovable and lovely.

Entering into a novel, the reader knows so little that they're uncomfortable, even squirmy or jittery. We're generous, us readers, and will give an author as many as fifty pages of suspicion before feeling secure in the major characters, settings, and themes. But one thing we will not put off is deciding who to root for.

I didn't know this was a rule until a teacher asked us to read the first page of ten novels at random. All the ones I read had a first-page scene in which the protagonist was complimented by another character. Maybe it was a random error, and this isn't a real rule, but I just tried it with

Conjugating Hindi by Ishmael Reed, and sure enough, tucked into the bottom of the first page describing the central character I found the phrase "He was popular among his students. . . ." That's definitely a character to cheer for.

Anne's take:

YOU, AS A WRITER, ARE ASKING US TO COME SIT BY THE campfire and listen to your story, and very few of us want to spend all that time with you if your character annoys us or puts us off. Remember: You need to get us to turn the page, and I am not going to keep reading if I don't like the main figure.

The wonderful novelist Ethan Canin, who taught for years at the Iowa Writers' Workshop, told me thirty-five years ago that the most important aspect of a novel was a likable narrator. Think of being led on a tour through a distant country: If the tour guide is learned but not likable, you're going to have a lousy time. You want someone at the helm who's worth spending time with. You like their vibe, their observations, and what they make of people and life; you like who they are and how they treat people. So it is with main characters: They can do terrible things and make awful mistakes, because otherwise there is probably no plot. But still, we have to want to spend time with them. Ignatius J. Reilly is a train wreck of a central character in

John Kennedy Toole's *A Confederacy of Dunces*, but a lovable train wreck.

(Now, by the same token, Ethan told me that same day that you should never write out of spite or revenge, while I have told oceans of students they need no other reason.)

RULE 28:

Once Is Enough

Keep your first description of a character or place distinctive enough that you aren't tempted to add to it later.

SOON AFTER ANY CHARACTER ENTERS, DESCRIBE THEM physically, in one concise paragraph. You won't need to ever again. Add an additional descriptor, or repeat one, only when it might help the reader, not to reinforce something you've already expressed. If he's a pirate with a hook for a hand, the hook will need to play a role in a pivotal action scene. But if she wears an eye patch, you might never mention it again.

This rule has an unfortunate corollary: You better spend a lot of time on that introductory paragraph. Each sentence in that paragraph will probably need to be revised and refined, changed and sorted, multiple times. The character's first entry needs to be memorable, both in psychological foreshadowing, and in their physical attributes. They can be short or tall, of course, or even medium height, but they also have to display either defects (a lopsided smile, or a slight crossing of the eyes, akimbo elbows), or striking affects (a lustrous gleam, imperceptible drool, charging walk), or admirable qualities (a swimmer's shoulders, honest hairline, confident jaw).

Here is the great short story writer Gina Berriault using one telling detail to fix a new character in our mind forever. It's all we know about this central character's looks: "His profile with that heavy chin that he liked to remind everybody was Hapsburg hung openmouthed against the blowing fog and the cold jet-black ocean of night."

And here's an example of a character's first description wandering through multiple aspects of his life and personality, from the second paragraph of Andrew Sean Greer's novel *Less*: "His slim shadow is, in fact, still that of his younger self, but at nearly fifty he is like those bronze statues in public parks that, despite one lucky knee rubbed raw by schoolchildren, discolor beautifully until they match the trees. So has Arthur Less, once pink and gold with youth, faded like the sofa he sits on, tapping one finger on his knee and staring at the grandfather clock. The long patrician nose perennially burned by the sun (even in cloudy New York October). The washed-out blond hair too long on the top, too short on the sides—portrait of his grandfather. Those same watery blue eyes." This might possibly not be someone to admire.

Keeping the telling detail in line with the personality reminds me of Anton Chekhov's weaponry rule: If a gun is mentioned, it has to be fired. Likewise, if my character has a faded look, at some point they have to fail.

Consider every prop, setting, expression, and character in your story as a clue. All novels are detective stories to the reader puzzling out the meanings. You can insert all the red herrings you want, but the more unusual the object or description, the more the reader expects it to fill an empty space in the compact puzzle that will be completed a little before the final page.

Anne's take:

I USED TO AGREE WITH NEAL ON THIS, AND THEN I GOT old. Now I am glad if a careful, respectful writer mentions important physical or historical details about a character more than once. In the first third of a novel, we have been introduced to a number of characters and are just coming to know them, and things can get muddled for me. I'll probably remember big deals about each person but maybe not some piece of connective or relational information between the people that factors significantly as the plot unfolds.

This is why you need a writing group or partner who will let you know that you already told them that, and it bugs them. Or they might say they would have liked to have been reminded that Julie's first of three marriages ended with the ex in jail, where she met her second husband in the visitor's holding pen, who was also visiting her ex, with whom he had dealt Quaaludes in college. Remind us in subtle, thoughtful ways, and then see what your writing friends have to say.

RULE 29:

Smell the Roses

Sight is only one of five senses; let your readers enjoy touch, hearing, smell, and taste.

GO BACK AND ADD THE SENSORY INFORMATION YOU left out: smells, flavors, feelings, noises. You're probably already perfectly good at providing the visuals. Most of us have memories that lean heavily on an internal movie screen. But living in the present isn't like that: We're taking cues from sounds, smells, and our tingling skin all the time, and then there's the taste of lamb korma! You want a seamless world? Evoke the rumbling train, the distant whistle, the neighbors arguing next door, the sweet fragrance of masa tortillas on any crumbled street in rural Mexico.

Humans rely more on visual cues than most other animals. Our sight is remarkable and can pick up extremely fine detail. On a dark night, our eyes can make out a lit match a couple miles away. This assists our hunting, our socializing through recognition of cultural and individual details, and our ability to travel long distances into new environments. A human eye can take in a million impressions at once. We get the big picture. We also hear well, through a broader spectrum of tonality than most creatures. But that reliance on sight backed up by sound means that our other senses—taste, touch, and smell—offer writers an opportunity to fulfill the reader's desire for novelty. If I'm not thinking about smell much in my daily life, the most familiar of odors can seem worth noting, even remarkable. A hit of gasoline at the pump. A sweet trace of bay leaf in the woods. A skunk prowling my yard? No, it's just my neighbor lighting up another skunkweed joint. Viewing the kitchen counter is mundane no matter how well written; smelling a strawberry-rhubarb pie pulls the reverse lever on the time travel machine. Proust didn't begin *Remembrance of Things Past* with a view of his room as a child, but with the taste of a madeleine.

Here is the famous passage:

> No sooner had the warm liquid mixed with the crumbs touched my palate than a shudder ran through me and I stopped, intent upon the extraordinary thing that was happening to me. An exquisite pleasure had invaded my senses, something isolated, detached, with no suggestion of its origin. And at once the vicissitudes of life had become indifferent to me, its disasters innocuous, its brevity illusory—this new sensation having had on me the effect which love has of filling me with a precious essence; or rather this essence was not in me it was

> me. . . . Whence did it come? What did it mean? How could I seize and apprehend it? . . . And suddenly the memory revealed itself. The taste was that of the little piece of madeleine which on Sunday mornings at Combray (because on those mornings I did not go out before mass), when I went to say good morning to her in her bedroom, my aunt Léonie used to give me, dipping it first in her own cup of tea or tisane. The sight of the little madeleine had recalled nothing to my mind before I tasted it. And all from my cup of tea.

The sight of the little madeleine had recalled nothing to my mind before I tasted it.

I make a separate pass through my fiction to add other senses in action, because I know I'm overly attached to visuals in my early drafts.

Senses can be found inside, too, in subtle touch and bouts of ordinary synesthesia. I don't just judge truth, I land in it, with a slight feeling of fullness in my lower belly or guppies rushing up my spine. A noisy cocktail party in a high-ceilinged room is metallic to my ears, while the seaside is scented with salted cod and boardwalk taffy.

Anne's take:

I LOVE THIS RULE AND I LOVE BOOKS AND POEMS RICH in sounds and tastes and touch. Smells are such profound links to memories. A lighted candle, your grandma's biscuits, honeysuckle, gunpowder, the night, the dawn. Once my very young son was riding on someone's shoulders late at night. He looked up at the sky and said, swooning, "It smells like moon."

So light a candle or get outside before the sun rises, and inhale deeply. Scribble down copious notes about the experience, although you will use only one sentence in your writing.

And touch, wow: the lawn and orange peel and the skin of the oldest and youngest people you know. Go get your silk blouse out of the closet, close your eyes, and feel its slinky smoothness. Find a burlap sack and a rose petal and a rock and your own hand: Close your eyes and let the descriptors come.

Read the masters and see how they do it, Hemingway and Fitzgerald and Mary Oliver and Terry Tempest Williams and Shakespeare.

Our senses ground us to this earth and to each other, and paradoxically, they are how our imaginations take flight. I am so grateful when a writer includes a lot of carefully chosen details about the world outside us, above us and below us and all around us, because then I see, hear, touch, taste, and smell those moments as if for the first time. They spritz me awake.

RULE 30:

Don't Filter

Don't point out that someone is thinking, opining, or experiencing what is already happening on the page.

THE LESS SELF-CONSCIOUS THE CHARACTER, THE MORE gripping. Don't start a sentence with "He thought" or "She wondered" or "They felt," or anything that filters the scene through a character's brain.

Staying on top of this rule takes more work than you might think. Our everyday conversation is littered with "I was wondering," "I feel like," "I hate it when," "I'm worried that," "I think that," and on and on. Dialogue in real life and on the page improves when we engage the thought as an activity. Often the way out is by the character asking a question: "What would happen if?" Sometimes the thought is just shortened: "That's right" instead of "I feel like you're right about that."

"Bruce, you're such a jerk," Mabel said. What follows are three possible responses by Bruce, in pairs. In each pair, the first one filters his response. Notice how much more the second version, without a filter, grabs you.

> He thought she was right.
> She was right.
>
> She is right, he thought.
> She is right.
>
> "I think you are right," he said.
> "You are right," he said.

As an author, your superpower of self-reflection can emerge as a pernicious obstacle. Watch out for it. Hide it. Thinking is the opposite of action. If you're writing nonfiction, action may not be the motion of a story, but of an argument. Self-reflection in the midst of a logical argument stalls out the same as in a car chase. All men are mortal. I *think* Socrates is a man. Therefore, I believe that Socrates is mortal. Huh? Because it is understood that thoughts and beliefs drive statements, presenting them in a sentence will be assumed to signal doubt. If that's what you want, fine, but otherwise try to scrap verbs of consciousness.

This is not a hard-and-fast rule. Sometimes it is perfectly appropriate to indicate that the character is musing.

There's even a corner of literary writing called metafiction or ur-fiction, which is intentionally self-conscious, to the point of elevating authorship to the surface. By layering in the author as a character, usually biased and therefore unreliable as a narrator, meaning is disrupted, which is a riddle of its own surrounding the more typical puzzles found in any novel. Masters at this such as Italo Calvino or Umberto Eco embrace the postmodern philosophers of the late twentieth century, and their works can be genius in elaborating the kinks and possibilities in meaning. But before trying it yourself, recognize how much they have demanded of themselves, and the reader, in order to retain seamlessness both of the traditional story elements and of the lurking presence of a philosopher masquerading as a narrator. They have entered a hall of mirrors that requires a rich understanding to navigate. I love to read them; I wouldn't dare imitate them.

Memoir and other forms of subjective nonfiction may also find verbs of opinion to be appropriate, especially in separating out facts from reflections. But even there, it might be wise to point out the subjectivity sparingly. The reader remembers.

Anne's take:

IF YOU ARE BLESSED SOMEDAY TO BE COPYEDITED BY A fierce, anorexic Croatian, as I was once, you will stop filtering your narration so often, or risk his contempt each time he catches you at it. If you can't break the habit, then go over your (theoretically) final draft and be on the lookout for verbs of opinion—"believed," "felt," "thought." You'll discover that you can take out a lot of them.

As Neal grudgingly acknowledges, you'll settle sometimes on a sentence where a character does wonder, feel, or believe this or that. Of his examples above, I would have had Bruce the jerk say, "I think you're right." This sounds more natural to me.

These rules were never meant to dress you as an exterminator, fixated on eradicating every adverb, every filtering word, every "very" and "it." Few of you work for Terminix. You work for you. The rules are simply suggestions for writing better sentences, clearer and more inviting.

With my fading memory, I recall a fashion icon suggesting that after getting ready for an evening out, you take off one thing—the brooch or the barrette, for instance, or the paisley pocket handkerchief. Obviously, certain events dictate that you wear a Last Supper cummerbund, and far be it from me, etc. Like most protocols, they apply to most of us, most of the time, in most circumstances.

Neal suggests in Rule 9 that you *question* transitions, and here the suggestion is that you *question* each filtering word. Leave in the ones that you like. Some tense, angry copy editor may some day attempt to change your mind, but don't forget whose work it is, and that you work for you.

RULE 31:

Trust Your Reader

Your reader will fill in the gaps; you only need to be complete enough.

IT'S WEIRD, BUT YOUR READER OF FICTION, MEMOIR, OR biography probably knows much more about your characters than you do. You've created what's actual and plausibly true to your character in the scenes of the book. Your reader fills in a lot of gaps. How many characters' ears have you described? If any, just the funny ones, I suspect. Your reader has sketched in the normal ears without prompting. Likewise, the reader constructs backstory and emotional characteristics that you haven't bothered about. Just like you in real life. If a stranger addresses you with a world-weary sarcastic demeanor, you might project on her a tough childhood or a past or present addiction. We all take tiny clues and blow them up into big stories. We're quite often wrong, but who cares?

All Hamlet has to say is "To be or not to be . . ." and we're off and running. He's overly cautious, so he probably didn't get a lot of direction from his father. Most likely he's not quite completely formed, and we can expect some juvenile behavior to come. Our interpretations are bound to be modern, informed by the post-Freud world, and psychologically grounded in the trauma theory of childhood. Harsh people come from dysfunctional families. Child abusers were abused as children. Good parents produce sweet children. Sociopaths emerge from violent backgrounds. These are tropes that the culture maintains, and even though they are unreliable (some sex workers have high self-esteem), the tropes are inserted by the reader when the backstory is left out.

Letting the reader fill in the gaps can be a lifesaver in the right hands—a novelist who can provide context and layering in other ways than backstory—or it can simply be laziness in the wrong hands, reducing characters to paper cutouts. Just because the reader is filling in the blanks doesn't let you off the hook.

Nothing wrong with being direct with the backstory. Here's most of the second paragraph of Dickens's *Great Expectations*:

> As I never saw my father or my mother, and never saw any likeness of either of them (for their days were long before the days of photographs), my first fancies regarding what they were like, were unreasonably derived from their tombstones. The shape of the

> letters on my father's, gave me an odd idea that he was a square, stout, dark man, with curly black hair. From the character and turn of the inscription, "Also Georgiana Wife of the Above," I drew a childish conclusion that my mother was freckled and sickly. To five little stone lozenges, each about a foot and a half long, which were arranged in a neat row beside their grave, and were sacred to the memory of five little brothers of mine—who gave up trying to get a living, exceedingly early in that universal struggle—I am indebted for a belief I religiously entertained that they had all been born on their backs with their hands in their trousers-pockets, and had never taken them out in this state of existence.

Anne's take:

REMEMBER SIXTY YEARS AGO HOW *MAD* MAGAZINE HAD its own illustrated clichés? "Nursing a pet peeve" showed a middle-aged man in an easy chair with a strange creature in his lap sucking on a bottle.

My own absolute pet peeve in literature is when crime novelists kill off the parents of the lead character in a car wreck. At least once a month, I make my husband stop whatever he is doing to listen to me read aloud: "Jill [or James or Philip or Grace] lost her [or his or their] parents in a car accident when she [or he or they] was [were] fifteen." This often comes up in dialogue when people have just met and are getting to know each other:

> "Where do your parents live?"
> "They died in a car crash when I was little."
> "Oh, I'm so sorry."
> "I was raised by my grandparents. They were wonderful and did the best they could . . ."
> "Were? Have they passed, too? Oh, no! Don't tell me . . ."
> "Yes, strange as it sounds, they too were killed in a car crash."
> "Jeez, so incredibly sad. Do you have siblings?"
> "Don't ask. I'll fill you in on the way to the restaurant. Let me drive."
> "No, no! I'm good."

Dead, absent parents are the novelist's way of saying, "Reader, fill in the blanks. I don't have the time or interest to introduce you to the parents. I already have enough characters on my hands."

RULE 32:

Layer Your Sentences

Sentences convey more than information; their other purposes must be tended.

IF YOU'RE WRITING STRICTLY FOR MEANING, THE paragraph can be your basic unit. But if your interest is good writing, then the unit is the sentence. No sentence can be bypassed as simply transitional. Each sentence must serve multiple purposes, including two or more of meaning, plotting, character, diction, rhythm, harmony, color, and seamlessness. For Annie and me as writers, our eyes are on constructing a sentence that does more than convey a simple meaning. Our sentences carry heavy responsibilities.

Read a little Chaucer and you'll get what I mean. By writing in meter, Chaucer has taken care of rhythm; his words have to fit into the scheme and also have to sound right, or seamless, without what's known as a false note. While bouncing to the beat, he draws highly distinctive portraits of lovely, flawed people who almost, but not quite, exaggerate our everyday weaknesses. We're meeting them in rooms and on trails that are carefully described in few words, adding color. And as a storyteller who plots well, Chaucer can't be beat. Seldom are we far from meaning, plotting, character, diction, rhythm, harmony, color, and seamlessness.

> *She has risen, and dressed at first light,*
> *For May will have no slothfulness a-night,*
> *The season pricks at every gentle heart,*
> *And makes it from its sleep begin to start,*
> *And says: "Arise, perform your observance!"*
> *And this made Emily rouse her remembrance*
> *Of the honour due to May, and so to rise.*
> *She was clothed fresh to watching eyes;*
> *Her yellow hair was braided in a tress*
> *Behind her back, a yard long, I guess.*
> *And in the garden, as the sun up-rose,*
> *She walked up and down, and as she chose*
> *Gathered flowers, mingled, white and red,*
> *To make a woven garland for her head,*
> *And sang like an angel, as she went along.*

This sentence-first approach is the primary distinction between ordinary writing and literary writing. Ordinary writing is explanatory or plot-driven or character-driven or style-driven, and its sentences hang on consistency of the book's singular purpose. You're not supposed to reread a sentence in a page-turner. Literary works—fiction or nonfiction—deserve time to be pondered over. What's going on in the sentence? Is it as simple as it seemed on my first reading? If the feeling is "How did the author do that?" or "How did the author think that way?" then you're reading a layered sentence. Sure, a good metaphor is a dramatic element. But it needs to be encased in a believable character's diction and serve a purpose of pushing along not just any old meaning, but one that is important to the plot. As in an earlier rule, bringing in new sensory information can often fatten up a sentence in a good way, connecting the sentence's usefulness for plot or character to a satisfying recognition by the reader of the novel's other charms—for instance, its seamlessness and color.

Layering your sentences means going back and looking at each one, asking, "Could it be more rhythmic, more psychologically astute, more sensory, more abrupt, more engaged in the plot, more characteristic of the player, more melodic? Is it doing two or more of those? Can I add one more?"

Of course the distinction between ordinary and literary writing is artificial. The tools of the high artist are available to the Sunday painter. No matter what I'm writing—a book or a business plan—my sentences can be better layered.

Anne's take:

I MAKE SENTENCES FOR A LIVING. AFTER I CREATE ONE decent sentence, I create another. Sentences are the beads with which I assemble the necklace of each paragraph and passage.

For example, I wrote a sentence in my late twenties with only six words, but what a story they foretold: "Against all odds, the cat lived."

Anyone in their right mind will think, "Oh, thank God," except for cat-hating spouses at their wits' end with the stench of the lion's den that seeps from the cat box. It's apparently a miracle, in six words. In fact, it was.

The star of the sentence, said cat, was a tabby who shared my houseboat on San Francisco Bay, and at that point, toward the end of my drinking career, existed in part as my main source of happiness. One day I came home from a walk to find her hunched over in a corner, her back to me, and upon closer inspection, discovered a gaping hole in her chest.

She was frozen, unblinking, barely holding on. I raced her to a pet emergency room, where the vet and I noticed after he soaked up the blood that we could see her lungs. (For the record, cat lungs are triangular, about the size of scones.) The vet did not think either had been punctured by whatever had pierced her chest, which was good news. The bad news? Splinters.

It was suggested at this point that I go wait at home, as

all the blood had drained from my face, in solidarity with the cat.

Against all odds, the cat lived. The vet surmised that she had leapt onto one of the pilings next to my houseboat, and that there must have been a sharp stick poking out of it. Somehow—and this was proof for me that there is a God in heaven—the stick had gone right between her lungs, missing both of them.

Also against all odds, I brought her home the next day. She was stitched and bandaged and pretty nonchalant about the whole thing—like, *whatev*. I would have milked this injury for months. She lived another ten years, long enough to help get me sober.

And I told you that story by creating one decent sentence after another, putting a period at the end of each one, pausing, looking it over to see if I could make it better, clearer, more visual, thereby advancing the plot and raising the stakes.

RULE 33:

Write the Hard Stuff

Don't shy away from the big mysteries of life.

NOTHING IS INEFFABLE. MAKE THE EFFORT: WRITE THE material whose articulation first stumps you, the stuff that makes people tick until the last tock.

Part of "show, then tell" is to stretch your imagination, whether it's heading into the physical world or abstract judgments of that world or painful emotions. If you stop at "She was beautiful in a vague way," you are giving up. It sounds kind of literary and meaningful, but lands to the reader as a cheat. If you stop at "He believed in God but wasn't sure which one," you're not allowing yourself to riff on the divine. If you stop at "The car was one of those cheap Indian things," you haven't completed your research on domestic car production in India.

An odd corollary is to force a little more simplicity on yourself. Yes, expressing the obvious is deadly. But so is ignoring the fundamentals that drive human behavior and emotion. Here's the twentieth-century philosopher Ludwig

Wittgenstein: "The aspects of things that are most important for us are hidden because of their simplicity and familiarity." Your characters have simple beliefs: *Nothing is as important as protecting my kids. Some people are just bad. Roses smell like Grandma. A wide panorama always reminds me of possibility.* Don't be afraid to punctuate a scene by expressing the obvious.

Finding a way to evoke the ineffable is related to Donald Murray's idea that "syntactic failure is a sign you're trying to say something important." In other words, if it's hard to write, it's probably worth writing.

Isn't the whole point of writing to figure out something you don't already know? Most fiction and biography writers discover aspects of their characters along the way. In general nonfiction, the author seeks motivations and causes of events. The act of writing refines the author's notions and often opens new possibilities. I once heard the novelist Siri Hustvedt complain that her protagonists keep getting killed off at the end of the story. She wants to protect her characters from themselves but can't.

In many traditions, God is expected to be so ineffable that it's hubris, even sin, to try to explain the concept. But those same traditions fill libraries with stacks of theology—the study of God. Don't pretend that anything is off-limits to your consideration and articulation. You go where your characters go, inside and out, in their metaphysical meanderings and hikes through the woods. Often nonfiction writers believe that they must wrap things up neatly and maintain an objective stance that might wobble if contaminated by subjectivity or the Great Irrational. Wittgenstein said, "The limits of language are the limits of my world." Well . . . my words include "mystery" and "supernatural" and my syntax includes questions and paradoxical statements. When I worked in daily newspapers, I could only ask a question that could be answered in the next paragraph. Magazine, blog, and book writers often restrain themselves the same way, but that's a shame. They have room and therefore license to raise the stakes, even if it makes some of their readers uncomfortable.

Here is novelist José Saramago on what's important about the hard stuff: "Inside us there is something that has no name, that something is what we are." While Saramago is claiming its unnameability, he is also tipping off his interest in the subject as an author. What does he care to write about? The ineffable.

And here's how you do just that, if you're Cormac McCarthy: "They were watching, out there past men's knowing, where stars are drowning and whales ferry their vast souls through the black and seamless sea."

Anne's take:

PLEASE PLEASE PLEASE WRITE THE HARD STUFF—WRITE about life, and death, and loss, and hope, and how on earth you survived that childhood or injury or marriage. Find a way to write about people's underlying fears, maybe psychological but also mystical—fear of death, of legacy, of emptiness and lovableness. Write about who you think you are down deep, past the persona and curation and the stories you believe about yourself, because you are probably similar to me, and I love it when someone holds up a mirror. I love revelation.

We're a species that craves stories about itself. Tell us our story, through your lens, whether in fiction or nonfiction. It is really all you have to offer us.

We are all going to die. (Hit the decks!) How do we live fully, boldly in the face of that? This is hard to think and write about, but we want you to. It is essential that you try.

We're here on the incarnational side of things to discover the truth of who we are. We're animal, human, divine. That is hard stuff to capture but that is what I most long to read: truth. Your truth; our truth.

Try. This will not go well, but don't give up. Write an incredibly shitty first draft that will be way too long and overwrought and sophomoric. Then take out all the boring parts and see what is left. Then try again and see if you can make it better.

Go deeper.

Talk to people about what you are working on and see if their input throws some lights on for you, or even provides phrases that will help you capture what you are after in your next draft.

(P.S. I've always said that if you want to be a writer, you should get the smartest, funniest friends, but it is best if they are not writers, too, because then they won't let you steal all their great lines about these profound matters.)

RULE 34:

Break the Rules

A rule may be of universal use, but need not be universally used.

AS I'VE SAID, THESE ARE TIPS, NOT RULES, UNTIL THE time that you decide to adopt them. But even then, they're not black-and-white like grammar. And at some point, you probably will need to break a rule—leave in a "very," keep a weak verb, stick with a Latinate noun.

My advice is to consciously practice each rule over and over at first. Know the rule backward and forward—trust its protective coating—before you test it and then break it. Relearn the rule after breaking it.

For the sake of argument, let's distinguish four ways we use words: to convey information, to narrate our own lives back to ourselves, to come to agreement, and to entertain.

Most communication is quite practical—giving directions, offering or receiving help or instructions, checking in, assessing health, those sorts of things. It's in that realm that the rules of grammar presumably developed.

The more practical the communication, the more narrow, repeatable, colorless, and recognizable it is. The rules of grammar you learned in class are the tightest set of rules of all. They are aimed at practical knowledge expressed through expository writing. The rules help make instructions clear and airtight. Good grammar narrows possibilities into a single, shareable meaning.

But most of the words going through my head aren't communicated to anyone else. They aren't purely instructive; they're often simply descriptive. I'm reminding myself of ongoing interests, worries, observations, and conclusions. Most of my thoughts are fragments that scarcely require grammar. I narrate my life with abandon.

Notice that one set of rules, highly constrained, establishes boundaries for writing that engages in exposition and the classic thesis-support paradigm, while a different set of rules, less constrained, allows in the fickle, free-verse meanderings of our internal narrative. Somewhere in between these two models floats creative nonfiction like memoir, or essays, or political speeches, or documentaries, or lyrics, which may have elements of practical knowledge and even wisdom, but also have distinct first-personalness that doesn't mind a little ambiguity or subjectivity. Whether writing in the first or third person, the first person is always implied in fiction. The author is not operating a mechanical conveyor of information. The author is replicating human consciousness, because we humans constantly think about things and sum up as we're experiencing things. Part of the realism of a fictional work is the reader's belief that the author is replicating the feeling of consciousness accurately. And consciousness does not speak to us in tidy, complete sentences. Consciousness is more than an instruction manual; it also loves the scalloped, spiky edges of an aloe plant. And it abets our desire for companionship, agreement, intimacy.

So fragments are allowed in fiction. Like this. But wait. This book is nonfiction, isn't it? How can I rationalize the incomplete "Like this"? Easy. I'm writing in a particularly conversational nonfiction style. It replicates a more typical style of fiction. I'm not actually breaking a rule. I'm turning on a different rule set, the rules of fiction. First-personalness. When we break the rules, often we're simply changing frameworks, maybe recognizing the entertainment value of drama.

My first professional writing was journalism. As a newspaperman, I learned how to write without reference to myself, in a straightforward way that mainly linked a lot of subject-verb-object sentences together.

A few months after leaving newspapers for a corporate career, I found myself writing a speech for the president of my company. Wow! Sentence fragments! First person! What was this? It felt like freedom! The rules were out the door! But in the words of every frowning eighth-grade teacher, with freedom came responsibilities. How to carry emotion without manipulating the truth? How to persuade rather than explain? In fact, I had to learn a new set of rules, and they were more subtle and more difficult.

Notice who your audience is and what the purpose of your writing is, and learn the rules that accompany those conditions. You may never need to break a rule again.

Anne's take:

THE FIRST RULE OF FIGHT CLUB, I MEAN WRITING CLUB, is you don't talk to yourself about the rules of writing. Just write and write and write. At some point, God willing, an editor and then a hidebound copy editor will step in and want you to stick to their rules, which maybe you will or maybe you won't. It is your material. Until then, just write the best you can, the way the words come through you.

You can break any rules that you can get away with. We've already discussed the rule against semicolons, and how often I use them (so they must be OK). We've gone over "show, then tell," and so forth.

Don't write in the second person? Tell that to Italo Calvino in *If on a Winter's Night a Traveler*—or to Lorrie Moore, who frequently uses second person in those wonderful early short stories.

Readers find patois and dialect annoying? Really? What about the great *Far Tortuga* by Peter Matthiessen, or *Train-*

spotting by Irvine Welsh, or *Their Eyes Were Watching God* by Zora Neale Hurston?

The most important thing in fiction is a likable narrator? What about Humbert Humbert in Nabokov's *Lolita,* and Merricat Blackwood in Shirley Jackson's *We Have Always Lived in the Castle?*

And speaking of Jackson, let's point out again that she said, "A confused reader is an antagonistic reader," and this in fact is the one rule I swear by as if written by the Psalmist. If I can't follow what you are up to in your first chapter, that is absolutely as far as I am going to read. Maybe I would have stuck it out for another few chapters in my younger days, when I was able to dive into a postmodern Japanese novel with some excitement, or William S. Burroughs, or Gertrude Stein. Nowadays, the princess does not do Dada. The princess wants you to tell me a rich, layered, and touching story.

RULE 35:

Finish the Damn Thing

Your job is to complete the project. The final quality and consequences are not yet your business.

FEAR OF FAILURE DRIVES PROCRASTINATION, WRITER'S block, and other forms of not-writing. A writing job requires a commitment, but that's not as big a deal as it sounds. The agreement to write the piece was made at the beginning. When I made that choice, I had factored in my time, my talent, my interest, and my ability to concentrate. None of those was in question. Only after jumping in do I start to doubt my time, my talent, my interest, or my ability to concentrate. But wait, I never choose a project that's over my head. People don't do that. Even when it's chosen for me by a boss, it's typically within my capacities. So if it's not over my head, then surely I can finish it. The base level of work called completion is already in the bag. Here's the only problem: My fearmongering inner critic has chosen to ignore that. The difficulty isn't my writing; it's the gremlin in my head.

As my buzzkill wife is known to say about the writer's life, "It's going to go badly." That's a given. I'm going to stumble into dead ends, difficult passages, unnecessary digressions, crummy sentences, lapses in logic, and every other kind of mind-twister. But I knew when I committed to the project that it would present obstacles. Big deal. So one way to address not-writing is to remember that it was never intended to be smooth; the logjams in the middle were always going to show up to be sorted out.

A peskier issue is removing concerns about quality and consequences.

Here's a thought: My job is to write the book. My editor's job is to worry about its consistency. My publisher's job is to worry about its sales. I can be interested in its consistency and sales, but they are not my responsibility, at least not yet.

First, quality: The funny thing about the sophistication of my ideas, language, and presentation is that those are a given before I start. I'm so used to the world telling me to improve myself that I don't notice that as an adult in the third third of life, I've already improved about as much as I can. At least 80 percent of the project's quality is already baked in before I start, because I have my acquired knowledge, my helpful and harmful biases, and my limits, none of which is going to change much over the course of completing the project. What if I didn't worry about quality while writing? What if I trusted myself? And when I've completed a first crummy draft and a second more polished draft, then maybe I can trust that it's ready for an editor. In the meantime I don't have to do the editor's job for her.

Second, sales: The publisher bought the book from me with an eye toward the maximum number of copies likely to be sold. After the editor has decided the book is ready for market, the publisher might assign me some promotional duties—social media posts, appearances, podcasts, workshops, networking—but *none of that is of any importance* during the period that I'm writing the book. Write first. Worry about promotion after. That's true for self-publishers, too.

Your job is to complete the current draft. That's all.

Speaking of completion, how do you know you've ended the book in the right place? Have you written a tragedy or comedy or something in between? The finale decides. Even if Orson Welles is right, and the relative happiness of a movie or book's ending depends on where you end it, make sure the final pages are gratifying to the reader. That means all escape routes seem closed; the denouement seems inevitable. C. S. Lewis said, "I sometimes think that writing is like driving sheep down a road. If there is any gate open to the left or the right, the readers will most certainly go into it." You've tied up loose ends without bringing in extra string. Whatever you do, don't introduce a deus ex machina, a convenient and magical solver of all problems, ten pages before the ending, in desperation to resolve things, quit writing, and get on with your life.

There is no worse ending for a crime novel than to discover after a dozen red herrings have been tossed aside that the culprit didn't mean to kill the victim; it was a head wound from an everyday bar fight. For some reason, TV scriptwriters seem to believe that this is OK once in a while. It is not.

Many fiction authors write without a preliminary outline. They let the story tell itself as it goes, and don't know where it will end until it does. Nonfiction writers have a similar experience when the book they proposed changes course as their research takes them down new channels into new revelations. Getting ahead of the story flattens the experience; let go of some of the outline and let it blossom.

Whether you're writing a novel or a biography or a news article or a personal essay or a screenplay, the temptation is often to rush the ending. The finish line promises a sense of accomplishment and rest. Lots of books close with little more than a succession of plot points, the author having decided that their riffing on ideas is useless once the consequences are set in stone. But since we grow up with a belief that tales conclude with moral statements, the ending is the perfect time to equivocate, and let the happy or tragic ending be resolved while continuing the discussion of life's ambiguities.

What author has more complete resolutions than Jane Austen with her happy marriages? But look at the very last paragraph of *Emma*:

> The wedding was very much like other weddings,
> where the parties have no taste for finery or parade;

> and Mrs. Elton, from the particulars detailed by her husband, thought it all extremely shabby, and very inferior to her own.—"Very little white satin, very few lace veils; a most pitiful business!—Selina would stare when she heard of it."—But, in spite of these deficiencies, the wishes, the hopes, the confidence, the predictions of the small band of true friends who witnessed the ceremony, were fully answered in the perfect happiness of the union.

The manners in this novel of manners are being questioned to the end!

One thing I love about Austen is that her characters grow more and more verbose as each of her novels proceeds. The author holds close to "show, don't tell" at the beginning, then loosens the straps as the book races to a conclusion, which slows things down and builds tension. Often characters who spoke curtly in the first third of an Austen novel become blowhard speechifiers toward the end. But we're so engaged we don't notice that Austen is in full riff mode toward the finale. Yes, you know the ending about fifty pages in, but by extending the torture, especially toward the end, you don't care. You just want to hear Austen's voice—her ideas, and her twists—ringing through the characters' dialogue and orations, consistency of diction be damned.

Anne's take:

THE BEST REASON TO FINISH WHATEVER YOU ARE writing is that everything inside you says not to. The worst inner voice, that of perfectionism, insists that your work is not going anywhere in its current form, and you should toss it out and begin something new, something that it will tell you in a few weeks is also not worth finishing.

Finishing your project is a subversive act. Maybe it turns out worse than you had hoped, too weak to submit to an agent or a quarterly, but finishing gave you a couple of advantages.

The first is that you have weakened and worn down the bad voice. You are the one who calls the shots now.

The second is that with a finished and possibly shitty first draft, you may now know what you were shooting for all along. OK, it wasn't what you have printed out and are reading with a sinking heart and chocolate cravings. But knowing what your writing isn't is part of how you find out what it is.

In *Bird by Bird*, I wrote about a painter setting out to capture his vision on a canvas, beginning with the upper-right quadrant. When he is done, he sees that it is not at all what he had envisioned, so he conceals it with white paint, and tries again, now knowing one thing that it isn't. The second time, he comes closer, but his concept and vision still evade him. With his third attempt, his canvas finally approaches not what he had first imagined, but something maybe better.

I don't mean that you don't put aside work when you have tried everything unsuccessfully to make it salable. I have given up on a number of essays and manuscripts over the years, after having finished them. Writing and writing again is how we writers practice scales, how we get better over time. When we commit to finishing our work, this forces us to stay at the keyboard, pushing on through to the end.

Think of finishing as a little like being in labor, where you realize ten hours in that you don't even actually like children. Breathe. Push.

Samuel Beckett said, "Ever tried. Ever failed. No matter. Try again. Fail again. Fail better." This is the way of most artists and writers. Not giving up or giving in, getting each day's work done, is the payoff, loosening us up, cortisone for the soul.

Now as to endings, what I'm about to say is extremely personal to me, and I'm sure if Neal and I were to discuss this, it would end in an ugly fight.

I *hate* sad or ambiguous endings. Please, for the love of God, don't end your work with a miserable outcome for the main characters, except for the villain. I don't see the point in keeping us at the campfire for 300 pages, caring for your characters, pulling for them to come through the drama of humankind, only to conclude with bad or sad news.

You might say that a sad ending is like real life half the time, to which I would counter, "Oh, really? I hadn't noticed." I read to get lost in a riveting story and good writing. I love plots most of all that involve people coming through difficult and deeply human circumstances, with, as Salinger's Esme put it, all their f-a-c-u-l-t-i-e-s intact, their hearts and spirits and senses of humor restored even if they (like the rest of us) face challenging futures. I don't want a story where God or Life or The Good have saved our characters from drowning, only to beat them to death on the beach.

Also, two-thirds of the way through any excellent book, I'm so grateful for the ride—the attention and clarity and beauty and tension that the author has provided—that I'm pretty easy at that point. Neal is right for once that you just want to stay in Jane Austen's company toward the end of *Emma* or any of her books. Of course, none of us can write like her, but we can all strive to be trustworthy and friendly narrators of the stories we seek to tell.

RULE 36:

Worship (Talented) Editors

Writing is collaborative, and editors save your skin.

EDITORS DON'T IMPROVE ME; THEY FILL IN MY BLIND spots. I can't improve much on the many years that have brought me here during the relatively short time I spend writing the book.

I'll probably always sport the same blind spots. I forget to move beyond visuals. My characters aren't paranoid enough, or are cardboard. My language turns flowery. I can only get a sentence so far along and then I run out of good ideas for refining it. But a good editor chimes in with further suggestions for some of my sentences, passages, and scenes. If I listen openly, I can have fun making changes.

My first reader is Annie. She gently points out phrases I might want to rework, and I dispute every one of them. "Oh, I thought of that, but no." "The flow would be lost." "I think I need that for later." Within twenty-four hours I come to my senses and make every one of her corrections.

Annie, who is more grown-up than I am, swallows whole most of my suggested changes for her work, having decided that she completed her part already—the first draft—and trusting that my role is different. She then applies herself to what she calls the dental draft.

When we show each other the improved sentence, the response is always the same: "Yeah, that works." Sentences work or they don't. When they're missing something, they don't work. When they're all put together, they work.

The scariest moment in our relationship descended in our third week dating, when Annie asked to read something of mine. While I could claim to be a writer because I had made a living from it, calling oneself a writer isn't the same as being a good writer. As Annie silently read my short story on the couch we shared, my insides scrambled. When she set it down and expressed satisfaction with my prose, I was relieved. But I remained skeptical until a few days later when she offered me a first pass at editing an essay of hers. No professional writer would offer an unskilled writer a piece to edit.

A daily newspaper forces real-time collaborations. Reporters and editors labor under deadlines that allow only one working draft that is manipulated in bursts as the clock ticks. Mistakes are removed (mostly) and, in the rush, also added. Injecting errors of fact is inexcusable, but arrogant editors often find other, acceptable ways to butcher copy, dragging down syntax, usage, and rhythm. I could respect an editor who made two improvements for every added defect, and if the ratio reached closer to 3:1, they had something to teach me. When I moved to the editing desk, I held a weekly writing session with my group of talented reporters. We six would each clip an article that another of us had published the prior week. The rule was to highlight one sentence or paragraph that we might all admire. The choice passage would be read aloud, and then the writer questioned on how they arrived at that clever wording. Together, we learned new rules by examining good writing, without ever criticizing or correcting. Anybody can find fault. When peers meet, though, they can search for mutual respect.

An untalented editor is worse than no editor at all. You won't feel protected from your blind spots, and you can't trust the suggested changes. If you don't happen to be married to a great editor, take the time to find one. A serious editor will always let you have your way with your natural voice, ideas, and the book's gestalt. An editor isn't there to alter your voice or change the impression that the work will leave or improve on the quality you brought to the work. What they can do is get that quality to appear consistently. They're there for blind spots, of which I have many, and they're angels as they swoop in on gossamer wings and delicately lift my dragging sentences into the air.

Anne's take:

IT IS NO EXAGGERATION TO SAY THAT GOOD EDITORS are 30 percent of the reason you love the work of the writers you do. They would never take this much credit, but it has been Neal's and my experience. You work your butt off trying to get your story just right, and then give it to a writing partner or friend, and they fashion the first edit. You're told that your lede is weak and that the first page reads like you are just clearing your throat, and that you should end the whole thing two pages or chapters before you do, but the structure is fine—or it isn't, but they have a suggestion—and of course there are way too many adverbs, and you have repeated yourself here, and here and here, and this sentence doesn't work . . .

Then you do (some of) what they've suggested because you trust that they are both tough and respectful and know what they are talking about. You absolutely cannot see your own blind spots and pontificating and showing off. After a while with a manuscript, you can't even see your typos. When you edit yourself, your eyes glance off the page because you've gone over it too many times.

Then maybe a publisher buys it! And you will be assigned to an editor. This is fantastic, kind of a miracle, but confusing, because you'd thought you were "finished."

Dream on.

Now your real, honest-to-God professional editor reads

it slowly and marks it up, and thinks evil thoughts about what would be a better way to introduce this or that, and how—no offense—you can definitely lose twenty-five pages in the middle. If it's a book, they write a long editorial letter with ten main points, all the things they found wrong, the things that could be better, a few solutions, and two or three things they especially like.

This moment, when you receive the editorial letter, is a real test of your mettle. Can you get past the lifelong resistance to authority, the hurt feelings, the *but but but* everyone told me it was good? Can you retain a little self-respect in the presence of someone correcting your many mistakes? Of course you can. And then you start to feel the kind of relief that is called a blessing. Because now you have a map and a little light to see by. Someone invested in you has given you their best expertise and writing advice on how to vastly improve an already good piece of work, how to make it cleaner and richer, how to bring forth depth and charm, how to keep your voice as clear and true as possible, and, of course, how to save you from embarrassment. You are the lucky recipient.

Trust them.

A Final Word

WHEN I WAS TWENTY-SEVEN, MY FRIEND AND BOSS TOM Geyer, who was president of a national newspaper chain, said offhandedly, "I think I would have liked a career as a hack writer." He had just promoted me into the business side of newspapers. Two years later, he offered me a huge new job, which would make me wealthy in a very short time. Instead I resigned to resume my poorly paid reporting career. Little did he know that he had sabotaged his own plans for me with a single unmemorable—to him—comment.

Since then, I've defined myself as a hack writer. I can write anything for anybody, for pay.

When she was twenty-seven, my wife was already recognized in a quite different writing category. No hack—she was several years into the life of a *literary* writer.

Despite living for decades in our different roles in the world—one of us a hack, the other a literary author—when we finally met in 2016 and gingerly passed each other the draft pages emerging from our current work, and then received them back littered with scratches and comments, we knew exactly what the other meant by their coded suggestions—"tighten this," "weak verb," "passive phrase," "add sensory material," "cut this."

These rules may not be as necessary as grammatical conventions, but they seem to be universal.

Agreement on what is true is more difficult than ever, and our words are suffering. The acceptability of a sentence now runs a gauntlet of fads, prejudices, and know-nothingism as emotions and arguments over beliefs terrorize us all.

Still, the rules in this book continue to aid my hack writing even as the audience for any piece of writing gets more judgmental and skeptical. These tips aid my wife's literary writing in exactly the same way, because they ring with the universal human experience. They may betray some old, seemingly outdated cultural accoutrements, but most of them have a counterpart in any language. These rules economize, favor the plainspoken and the specific, keep the reader's attention sharp, and in other ways show respect for the audience's time and desire for novelty. They're not just for professional writers. A politician or lawyer can turn to these same rules of rhetoric, as can a lyricist, a teacher, or a family storyteller.

The ancient Greeks recorded the orations of Pericles and the dialogues of Socrates with the reverence and sense of immortal remembrance that caused the Egyptians to build pyramids. Americans connect our ideals to the persuasively written Declaration of Independence, preamble to the Constitution, and Gettysburg Address, the last one read aloud at least once by nearly every schoolchild in my day. Likewise, Britons quote Churchill and Shakespeare, Chinese Confucius and Mao, South Africans Mandela and Tutu, Iranians Mohammed and Rumi.

Our collective interest in elegant writing shines through the irony we all recognize in Lincoln's famous words: "The world will little note, nor long remember what we say here." Not true. For one thing, the Gettysburg Address is literally carved in stone at the Lincoln Memorial.

In the twentieth century, the word "rhetoric" lost its luster, tarnished by the modern malevolence of propaganda and Madison Avenue. But that misses the point. Writing in a way that persuades your reader to continue reading is not the devil's work. Persuasion, including the rhetorical devices, is separate and distinct from dogma, control, competitiveness, and emotion. It is true that these rules can be employed for thought control and advertising, but they work just as well in works of touching love and happy agreement. It is exactly that impartiality that gives them their universality, and when things are truly common among humans, we can trust them.

Now writing is being altered even more. I'm not convinced that books will survive the next few generations. Communication of knowledge and ideas has been transformed by technology and the common library called the

Internet. Clicking through websites has largely replaced ferreting out bits of information hidden in the pages of books. The new way takes seconds; the older one took hours. Maybe books of fiction will survive, but surely not practical nonfiction.

Ah, but these rules of good writing don't exist only on the written page. They inform all types of communication, including everyday speech. We enjoy being entertained and persuaded in conversation, on film, through headphones, in private, and out in crowds. Instead of reading, people are listening—to books, yes, but also to experts on podcasts. As those experts script or improvise their words, they're following many of the rules of rhetoric and persuasion that lifted Pericles two millennia ago and later, Shakespeare. Strong verbs keep the listener's attention exactly the same way they keep the reader's. I can't prove it, but I tend to believe that the rules of persuasion and sentence-making will survive any changes in media, and may always assist us in refining the words we use to understand the human experience.

Anne's take:

THE MODERN ERA IS SWAMPED WITH SO MUCH MURK and bullshit that when a writer finds the words and figures of speech to convey truth, and entice me into their story, I enter gratefully. When a writer chooses a verb that is so precise that it makes me look up from the page with admiration, I'm going to keep on reading. When a writer presents me with a tightly edited piece of work where they have clearly taken out all the boring and show-offy parts, this is work that I may very well foist on others.

My poor husband suffers from being gravely overeducated, and so I suggest that you gloss over the above references to Socrates and Pericles and focus instead on the seminal idea of his book: "These rules economize, favor the plainspoken and the specific, keep the reader's attention sharp, and in other ways show respect for the audience's time and desire for novelty."

Neal shared these thirty-six rules with me on our fourth or fifth date, and while their simplicity and brilliance were not the main reason I agreed to marry him a couple of years later, they didn't hurt. His rules helped me become a better writer, and if you follow them, your writing will get better, too. Your work will get more economical, sharper, and more riveting. It is possible that it will become both more fun for us to read and more fun for you to write. Our hope is that you will be able to edit your work in a more focused and efficient way. Long, boring descriptions, out; generic verbs, out; endlessly inserted adjectives and adverbs, out out out. And clichés, feh! You can do better.

I think in terms of three drafts. I start with a shitty first draft, then a much tighter second draft, and finally the dental draft. I have these rules in the back of my mind with the shitty first draft but do not bog down in perfectionism. I bring them forward somewhat for the second draft, being stricter about adverbs, adjectives, and excessive details. But the third draft is when I bear down on the work, tooth by tooth, sentence by sentence, poking and jiggling, and these rules are the tools for the cleaning, the drilling, the filling, the polishing.

Neal's bossy rules about what constitutes good writing can get you to hold yourself accountable, and this is good for any writer. Commit to spending the time it takes to find the exact right words, phrases, and descriptions that best express your creative intention, and, paradoxically your work will become freer, looser, and truer.

Discipline, in my experience, is what leads to freedom. I hope these rules and meditations serve as a guide and structure on which to base or improve your writing, as they have for me.

Writing is hard for people like me. Neal, who began as a journalist, sits down to write what is on his mind—novels, nonfiction, short essays—and just does it, as if he is still on deadline and the editor in chief is breathing down his neck. I feel more like Cindy Lou Who, tiny and vulnerable and brave. Everything I write takes several drafts, and the first one is always unreadable, even as its completion is a small miracle of determination beating back self-doubt.

This is where these rules make a difference: Every first

draft of mine is way too long, as in, for example, the year-long series of pieces I wrote for *The Washington Post* on being older. I was given 1,000 words. I would write 1,800, including many long elegant literary descriptions. Rule 7 reminds me that if it sounds literary, it isn't, so I would take (most of) them out, begrudgingly. Now the piece might be 1,600 or so words. Rule 14 encourages me to take out the boring parts, so there go another 300, mostly descriptions of nature or my own disappointing state of mind.

Next to go are many adjectives, adverbs, filtering words, and clichés. Then I remember an admonition of the legendary movie producer in early Hollywood Samuel Goldwyn, "If you have a message, send a telegram," so I take out (many of) the messages. Finally, with disappointment over how much of my deathless prose has been lost, I hand it over to Neal, which brings us to Rule 36: Worship (Talented) Editors. Believe me, at this point, with maybe 1,175 words left, there is nothing else that can possibly go. Right?

Not right. Neal comes back in half an hour with the marked-up pages. He says something along the lines of how he is going to love it with a little bit of cutting and jiggling, which means it is terrible as is.

We sit down together and look at his illegible markings. He thinks the entire first paragraph can go, a paragraph I worked on for an hour. "Hmmm," I respond, with indifference and contempt.

But I keep going.

And soon we're off and running, collaborating pretty excitedly, with him pointing out weak verbs and the need for better transitions from one point to the next, and ideas he has for additions (which may in fact be good, although they necessitate cutting out more of *my* words, which he has thoughtfully done).

This is what it takes for me to hand in my best possible work to my official editors, who then burnish it even further. I wish I were more like Muriel Spark, the prolific British writer who was said to feel so plugged in to God that she sat down to write feeling like she was taking dictation. I have never once in forty-five years had this experience, nor, for that matter, would I ever be close to a person who would announce this, no matter if it was true. The rest of us flail and slog and write terrible first drafts, and then we make them better. We do this because we're writers. It helps to accept that writing is 80 percent stalling, 10 percent laundry, and 10 percent struggling to capture ideas, experiences, and imagination in words. Sometimes when I want to give up, I remember being in labor. Everything painful feels good when it's over. Plus no one cares if we write or not, so we damn well better.

I do care that people write *well*, because of my starvation for truth, and for the joy of reading. Good writing has been my rock and salvation since my parents first read to me. Tonight when I crawl into bed, a good book is waiting for me, in which I will get lost and found. Neal will be there, too, also lost in a book, and we will be in peace. Suddenly, one of us will exclaim—I mean "say" (Rule 4)—"Listen to this," and then we'll read a sentence or description to each other, and shake our heads at how fine it is.

You are fully capable of creating good sentences, too, with practice, guidance, an editor or writing partner, and dedication to the craft. Trust me on this, but better yet, trust yourself: You've got this.

Neal's Kit Bag

The 36 Rules

1. USE STRONG VERBS: Replace weak verbs, which are imprecise ("walked," "stood"), with vivid verbs, which are specific ("trudged," "malingered").

2. QUESTION "BEING" AND "HAVING": The verbs "to be" and "to have" are the weakest of all; by nature static, they slow a narrative.

3. KEEP IT ACTIVE: Pay attention to words that end in -ed or -en and are preceded by a form of "to be," and watch out for -ing endings; try flipping the sentence to get it more active.

4. STICK WITH "SAID": When attributing a quote, "said" is the default verb; the reader's attention is on who said it, not how it was said.

5. DON'T SHOW OFF: Let others be erudite; your job is to befriend your reader.

6. PREFER ANGLO-SAXON WORDS: Favor shorter, punchier Anglo-Saxon words over fancy, abstract Latinate words.

7. SOUND NATURAL: Unless you're writing a technical manual, keep your language conversational and use modern speech patterns.

8. TRUST YOUR VOICE: Your natural voice has its own tempo, pitch, ease, and overall sound. Let it ring out.

9. QUESTION TRANSITIONS: Transitional phrases ("then," "next," "when," "meanwhile," "however") are not needed unless a gap in time or logic has opened.

10. LINK IDEAS WITH SEMICOLONS: If two sentences are tightly linked and one progresses from the other, consider separating them with a semicolon.

11. DROP "VERY" AND OTHER CRUTCH WORDS: The word "very" seldom improves a sentence.

12. JETTISON [ALL THOSE] TINY WORDS: Remove the clutter of short words (pronouns, prepositions, connectors).

13. DRESS UP "THIS": Pronouns are hard for readers to follow, especially "this" and "it."

14. REMOVE THE BORING STUFF: Spend less time defending what you've written, and more time revealing the truth.

15. REFRESH YOUR WORDS: Don't repeat a distinctive word unless you must.

16. KNOW YOUR WORDS INSIDE AND OUT: Examining the etymology of words makes them more concrete and useful.

17. STAY IN TUNE: The better word is both precise and unnoticed. A thesaurus is your book of magic spells.

18. FIND THE HIDDEN METAPHOR: Metaphors mirror humdrum experiences through elegant comparison. In the hands of an expert, they both illuminate and offer depth of field.

19. TWIST CLICHÉS: We already think in clichés; you owe it to your reader's search for novelty to remove or deconstruct your hackneyed phrases.

20. KNOCK THREE TIMES: For a series of terms to land, you usually need three.

21. STRETCH OUT: Long sentences require attention to detail, conjunctions, and rhythm—and a payoff at the end.

22. SHORT SELLS: Interrupt lyrical or otherwise long passages with an abrupt, short sentence.

23. GIVE YOUR SENTENCE A FINALE: Even if you begin your sentence with a punch, end it stronger.
24. CRYSTALLIZE YOUR DIALOGUE: Dialogue needs to be as zippy and economical as the rest of the book.
25. IN FICTION, ARCHETYPE YOUR CHARACTERS: Below the human stereotypes are common psychological patterns that readers expect.
26. SHOW, THEN TELL: Start with the concrete—what happened—and after, when appropriate, riff on your thoughts about consequences.
27. GIVE THEM A HERO'S WELCOME: Start off by telling the reader who to root for.
28. ONCE IS ENOUGH: Keep your first description of a character or place distinctive enough that you aren't tempted to add to it later.
29. SMELL THE ROSES: Sight is only one of five senses; let your readers enjoy touch, hearing, smell, and taste.
30. DON'T FILTER: Don't point out that someone is thinking, opining, or experiencing what is already happening on the page.
31. TRUST YOUR READER: Your reader will fill in the gaps; you only need to be complete enough.

32. LAYER YOUR SENTENCES: Sentences convey more than information; their other purposes must be tended.

33. WRITE THE HARD STUFF: Don't shy away from the big mysteries of life.

34. BREAK THE RULES: A rule may be of universal use, but need not be universally used.

35. FINISH THE DAMN THING: Your job is to complete the project. The final quality and consequences are not yet your business.

36. WORSHIP (TALENTED) EDITORS: Writing is collaborative, and editors save your skin.

Acknowledgments

NEAL: My bedroom shared the basement with my dad's small but sublime fiction library, a wide bookcase that loomed over the pool table. These few hundred dark cloth-bound books, dust jackets torn or discarded, opened their leaves to me as a beginning, as my guidance, my standards, and my expectations for my formative reading. It was a random rainy day in 1962 when I pulled down Irving Stone's *The Agony and the Ecstasy* to see what was going on in these fat, small-type, mysterious adult books. Without ever being told to, I let my dad's library take over as curator, my tastes over the next ten years refined by his literary heavyweights—Shakespeare, Joyce (Dad had read everything, even *Finnegans Wake* and *Stephen Hero*), Faulkner, Hemingway, Twain, Austen, Henry Miller, Sinclair Lewis, Salinger, Katherine Anne Porter—and, osmotically, my own writing improved. That's right. Read well and you'll write well. Pore through literary fiction and the possibilities of sentences open up. Thanks, Dad, and also for you and Mom, both trained copy editors, correcting our grammar at the dinner table. Rules are easier to retrieve when they're stored young.

Most of the guidance in the book was delivered to me in cursory and curmudgeonly form at deadline by editors and fellow reporters in my newspapering days. These ad hoc word coaches included Rob Borsellino, Sam Daleo, Jim McGarvey, Meg Lundstrom, Dean Chang, Manny Mendoza, Lucy Lu, Craig Gilbert, Mikhail Horowitz, Kent Allen, and of course many I've forgotten. Finally, forty years ago, Marilynne Robinson encouraged me on long sentences, on describing the supposedly ineffable, and on trusting my voice.

Writing professor Alexandra Youmans was instrumental in this book finding its way. Working with an early draft, she provided several of the examples sprinkled in, and introduced me to the "Unadorned This" demon that became Rule 13.

ANNE: My father, Ken Lamott, was a great writer. He taught me how to write, how to put into words what I saw, thought, and imagined, starting at an early age. He taught me the habits of writing, of sitting down at the desk at the same time every day, no matter what, and to keep working on my material until I got it right, got it to be the best I could muster, and then to do one more draft. He helped me learn to read and love poetry, to read great books to see how it was done, to immerse myself in the beautifully written word. He taught me that getting to write was a privilege. He is the reason I got to be a writer, too.

BOTH OF US: We adore and admire our agent, Sarah Chalfant of the Wylie Agency, who found us the perfect editor and publisher, Tracy Behar of Penguin/Avery.

As a collaborative entity, we each thank the other for their love, humility, and expertise. It never fails to surprise us the luck of finding an expert, friendly editor in-house.

Index

INDEX

INDEX

INDEX

INDEX